Battleground Europe
COURCELETTE

Battleground Europe
COURCELETTE

Paul Reed

Series editor
Nigel Cave

LEO COOPER

Dedicated to Yves Foucat, of Pozières
1929 - 1997

First published in 1998 by
LEO COOPER
an imprint of
Pen Sword Books Limited
47 Church Street, Barnsley, South Yorkshire S70 2AS

ISBN 0 85052 592 6

A CIP catalogue of this book is available
from the British Library

Printed by Redwood Books Limited
Trowbridge, Wiltshire

For up-to-date information on other titles produced under the Leo Cooper imprint,
please telephone or write to:

Pen & Sword Books Ltd, FREEPOST, 47 Church Street
Barnsley, South Yorkshire S70 2AS
Telephone 01226 734555

Cover painting: **A Tank In Action** *by John Hassell (1868-1948)*
Reproduced Courtesy of the Lincolnshire County Council: Usher Gallery

Puchevillers Cemetery in 1919, where many pre-Courcelette Canadians were buried.

CONTENTS

Canadians fighting at close quarters in front of the sugar refinery at
Courcelette.

PREFACE

The Somme continues to remain one of the most popular areas along the old Western Front for pilgrims to the battlefields. Come the summer almost every other car on the Albert-Bapaume road is British, tracing grandfathers and, increasingly, great grandfathers who served in the battle. Time and again such visitors see the same places - there is almost an accepted list of them. And one date obsesses them all - 1st July 1916. At times the casual visitor might be forgiven for thinking that the battle began and ended on that date. But the Somme slogged on until November 18th; beginning in the heavenly weather described by Siegfried Sassoon and ending in a snowstorm which blotted out the landscape.

Courcelette is one of those places on the Somme battlefields often overlooked by the summer visitors. Indeed, a member of the Western Front Association asked me during the research for this book, 'Did anything ever happen at Courcelette?' He went quiet when I mentioned 24,000 Canadian casualties, three Victoria Crosses and over two months of fighting.

Courcelette was indeed primarily a Canadian battlefield, but today few Canadians have either heard of it or come this way. Vimy overshadows the sacrifice on the Somme, and there is nowhere near the interest in things Great War in North America as there is, for example, in Britain or Australia. One can only hope this changes.

The joy of the *Battleground Europe* series of guides is that they provide answers to the sort of questions my WFA friend posed. Here the Courcelette volume covers the fighting for the village from the first attack with tanks on 15th September to the murderous fighting for Regina Trench to the final push on Desire Trench at the end of the Somme Battle.

Today the fields around Courcelette are silent. Occasionally, staring across the chalk downlands on the Ancre heights, one might hear the faint whisper of echoes past on the wind; talk of Jimmy Richardson piping his men into action, of Lieutenant Howard alone and surrounded, fighting to the last, or of Canon Scott making the long search for his son's grave at Regina Trench. There are countless stories. Many have their memorial in stone - what they did has never before appeared in print. So here, at last, I would like to hope the memory of them and the other 8,000 Canadian soldiers who fell on the Somme is not forgotten.

Paul Reed, Sussex & The Somme. Autumn 1997

Introduction by Series Editor

The Somme village of Courcelette was a place of considerable importance to the Germans from the time that the line stabilised in the area in 1914. One of its most important features was the large sugar refinery that was built there in the early years of the twentieth century. The only remnant of this place may now be found in the garden centre that is to the south west of the village, on the north side of the Albert-Bapaume road. In the grounds of the centre may be seen the top of the workings of the shaft that was sunk to provide the many gallons (or perhaps one should say litres) of water that were required for the refining of the beet. Its significance for the Germans was that this plentiful supply of water could be pumped forward to trenches and strongpoints in a part of France where water supplies are notoriously difficult. Indeed one of the reasons for the paucity of individual farms and instead their clustering into the typical Somme village is so that this water problem could be resolved by the use of communal wells and, in more recent years, water towers.

Courcelette is a most important place in the development of Canada's military history. It was here that the fourth Canadian division finally came into the same sector as its three fellows, although not for long; the final joining was to come in the winter of 1916 as the Corps took its position on the slopes of Vimy Ridge. Just as war often speeds social and technological change, so also it increased the speed of the political development of Canada as an independent nation, able to take its place in the councils of war and to follow a policy, if necessary, of its own.

The actions at and around Courcelette between mid September and mid November cost the Canadians just over 24,000 casualties; the nature of the battlefield was such that many of those who were killed in the fighting never received a proper burial – or if they did, they were often unidentifiable. Thus many of those who died here are commemorated on the monumental walls at Vimy; and a visit to that place and the recently opened (November 1997) Visitors' Centre, which attempts to explain the origins and recruitment of the Canadian contingent as well as the action at Vimy, is strongly recommended.

Paul Reed has the great advantage of living in Courcelette, and his house (which is also run as a Bed and Breakfast establishment) provides easy access to the killing fields around and about. Now they are quiet – a landscape that is quite bleak, with the customary open and vast fields that are a characteristic of this part of France. In the winter months, on a cold, bleak and foggy day it is not difficult to recreate an atmosphere (minus, of course, the stench of the dead and of cordite and the sound of the guns and small arms fire – and of the danger that they presented) which Canon Scott might have faced when he went out amongst the destroyed fields to look for the broken body of his son.

This is the second book in the Battleground series on the Somme to break out from the old 1 July start line. It illustrates something of the development in the thinking of the British army as it struggled with the reality of its first long, slogging major offensive against the might of German arms. The limited offensives that were now taking place in the later stages of the Somme required new skills in artillery and the management of the guns; in supplies; in infantry tactics and in reaction to those methods used by the Germans. Courcelette also witnessed the first use of tanks, admittedly in penny packet numbers, but that was to a large extent perforce. These great, unwieldy, cumbersome beasts, as far from their present descendants as the flintlock is from the self loading rifle, have their strangely effective memorial just outside Pozières, on the Albert-Bapaume road, on the high point, marked so conveniently by a large radio mast, one of the great marker points for those visiting the battlefield to-day.

I cannot let this opportunity pass without paying tribute to a person who features prominently in this book. Lance Cattermole served as an underage soldier in the CEF for a catalogue of reasons which I suspect

The tank was the chief innovation contributed by the British during the war. The scene below is after the action on the Somme in September 1916,

**The Tank Corps Memorial, outside Pozieres on the Albert-Bapaume road.
The photograph was taken in 1922.**

were quite common to many in that army. I had the privilege of knowing him for a few years before his death in the 1992. Anything more unlike the caricature of a Canadian lumberjack or Mountie it would be difficult to find; a quiet, articulate, cultivated man, who made his living from his art, most notably his painstaking recreation of the uniforms of the British army and empire. His wife Lydia maintains the contact, and I enjoy my periodic whiskey with her. It was a privilege to know veterans like Lance, acquiantanceships that I made in the early 80s and alas now all but gone, victims of time. They were not necessarily great men – but they had shared in a great experience, and were willing to share it with other, later, generations, people striving to understand something of what had happened so many years ago.

These men can talk no more, but it is the objective of books in this series, admirably carried out in this book, to try and ensure that what happened here in the fields, the ridges, the valleys and the byways of the Somme should not be forgotten; and to help people, however inadequately, to understand something of the who, the why and the wherefore, at least on the small scale of particular parts of the battlefield.

Nigel Cave, Ely Place, London

9

ACKNOWLEDGEMENTS

My old friend Tom Gudmestad, of Seattle, USA, proved his worth time and again by supplying me with copies of a mass of Courcelette material from his extensive archive of books, photographs and ephemera. Tom's knowledge of the CEF battlefields is second to none, and I hope that one day he will share that knowledge with us in the form of his own book.

The only veteran I knew who served at Courcelette was Lance Cattermole of Worthing, Sussex. Like all old soldiers Lance has 'faded away' but he left us a harrowing account of his service on the Somme – which is reproduced here with the kind permission of his family.

Others who have helped in a multitude of ways include: Paul Bardell, Roger Davies, Tom and Janet Fairgrieve of Delville Wood, Margery Giles for permission to use John's aerial photographs, Captain John Haslam CD of Newcastle, Ontario, Clive Harris, Mr G. Kingsley Ward of the Vimy Ridge Group, Matthew Richardson of the Liddle Personal Experience Archives, Tim Richardson, Klaus Spath, Frank & Lou Stockdale, Ed Storey of Kingston, Ontario, Julian Sykes, Trevor Tasker, Tom Tulloch-Marshall, Pam Waugh and Terry Whippy.

In France my thanks goes to Yves Foucat of Pozieres, who sadly died during the preparation of this book. Yves worked for the CWGC for forty-three years, and spent much of his spare time and retirement acquiring a knowledge of the Somme battlefields that is difficult to quantify – in particular he knew the Mouquet Farm-Courcelette area very well. I, and many other English visitors, learnt much from him. For me he was good friend of some fifteen years, particularly so to my family since we bought our house at Courcelette, and his wife continues to be so. We shall all miss him.

In Courcelette itself I am very grateful to my fellow villagers, who are always friendly and interested, and supported the writing of this book fully. In particular I would like to mention the mayor, Monsieur Philipe Gonse, whose family have owned Mouquet Farm for many generations, and Xavier Vandendriessche, whose father was born at Mouquet before the Great War, and sold us our house in Courcelette. Monsieur Gonse shows great interest in the history of his village, and recently donated a large piece of ground at Mouquet Farm to the Australian government so that a new memorial could be erected there. This was unveiled in September 1997.

The team at Pen & Sword also deserve mention, for help on this and my previous book. Roni Wilkinson in particular performs miracles with his DTP and I would like to thank him especially for all his good humour and assistance.

The staff of the Public Record Office have put up with my frequent demands and requests for material over many years. William Spencer in particular is always willing to share his knowledge of the records. At the Canadian National Archives in Ottawa, Ms Helen De Roia of the Reference Services was extremely helpful with requests for official photographs. Those members of the Commonwealth War Graves Commission who tend the cemeteries in and around Courcelette merit their own special acknowledgement for the dedicated work they do to keep these gardens of peace in such immaculate order.

Finally, my love and thanks to Kieron and Ed, who have walked the ground at Courcelette with me so many times and were willing to share the dream of owning a house on the battlefields, despite all the odds. This book is for them, and for our village – Courcelette.

ADVICE FOR TRAVELLERS

The Somme Battlefield is one of the easiest to reach from the channel ports and the tunnel. The motorway starts both at the Channel Tunnel and at Calais Port, and the Bapaume exit is reached within an hour and a half. Courcelette is then only a quarter of an hour away by the main road which runs from Bapaume to Albert. Indeed, Courcelette is almost in the centre of the 1916 Battlefields and is never far away from the many sites covered by other *Battleground Europe* guides. For those without transport, a train service runs from London to Amiens, where another train can be caught for Albert. But beware – local trains in France are few and far between. There are no local buses on the Somme, but a taxi service is available by the railway station in Albert. An overnight coach from London to Amiens is the most inexpensive way to reach the Somme. Cars are available for hire in Amiens, and bikes in Albert.

Accommodation poses few problems. In Courcelette itself, the author's wife runs an inexpensive Bed and Breakfast, which is in walking distance of all the places mentioned in this guide. Contact Ms Kieron Murphy at 'Sommecourt' on Tel/Fax (0033) 3.22.74.01.35. In nearby Martinpuich another English couple have recently opened up a Gite de France Bed and Breakfast, offering a variety of accommodation options, including full board. Colin and Lisa Gillard can be contacted on Tel/Fax: (0033) 3.21.50.18.87. At Pozieres, the enterprising Dominique Zanardi has transformed a local bar into 'Le Tommy' with many Great War exhibits, maps and photographs. He offers inexpensive lunches and from 1998 will have rooms available. Tel: (0033) 3.22.74.82.84. A number of similar B&Bs exist in the Somme area, and in Albert there are several good hotels, with many more in Amiens. Camp sites are found in Albert, Authuille and Miraumont. Information on all these can be found in the Tourist Office opposite the Basilica in Albert.

The Somme has two main museums. In Albert the underground Musee des Abris (Tel: 0033 3.22.75.16.17) has an excellent display of uniforms, weapons, maps, photographs and other artefacts. It is open every day from 10 am to 6 pm, but closes for lunch 12-2pm in winter months. Safe battlefield souvenirs are on sale here. In Peronne the Historial de la Grande Guerre (Tel:0033 3.22.83.14.18) is a very modern museum with much audio-visual material. It is open every day from 10am to 6pm but, as with the museum in Albert, opening times vary in the winter months. The souvenir shop here has a good range of books in French and English, and takes major credit cards.

The weather on the Somme can vary a great deal and a good waterproof and strong shoes are never wasted in the out of season

The 'Iron Harvest' at Courcelette 1997. Just some of the many types of shells found by farmers in and around the village. This pile included several gas shells.

months. In the summer there is little protection from the blazing sun in the open fields and a hat, sun cream and sunglasses are equally wise – as is extra water on a very hot day. A small walker's rucksack to carry your gear in is a good idea. Provisions can be bought in either Albert or Bapaume – Courcelette is roughly equi-distant from them both. The Visitors Centre at nearby Delville Wood, Longueval, offers liquid refreshments and snacks along with a good range of Great War books, maps, postcards, stamps, films and guides – and safe battlefield souvenirs. The complete *Battleground Europe* series of books is also on sale here.

The Courcelette battlefield, like any other area of the Somme, is littered with unexploded munitions of all types, which are still deadly and should be left well alone. Dumps of old shells and grenades can be found in at least two places in the village – by all means photograph and look, but do not touch! Each year people are maimed and killed while tampering with the so-called 'Iron Harvest'; in late 1996 three members of the Somme Bomb Squad were killed by Great War shells that exploded after eighty years in the ground.

The farmers in Courcelette are among the friendliest you will find on the Somme, and welcome British visitors. However, do bear in mind that crops can be damaged by walking on them, and that private property and people's personal privacy should be respected at all times.

For those with more than a passing interest in the Great War, membership of the Western Front Association is essential. Founded by author John Giles in 1980, the WFA now has branches all over the United Kingdom, and indeed overseas – some of which meet on a monthly basis. The annual subscription includes copies of the in-house newsletter, *The Bulletin*, and the glossy magazine, *Stand To!* Members also have access to the WFA's collection of trench maps and cheap photocopies of them are available – including several of Courcelette and Regina Trench. For further details contact:

The Western Front Association
PO BOX 1914
Reading
Berkshire
RG4 7YP

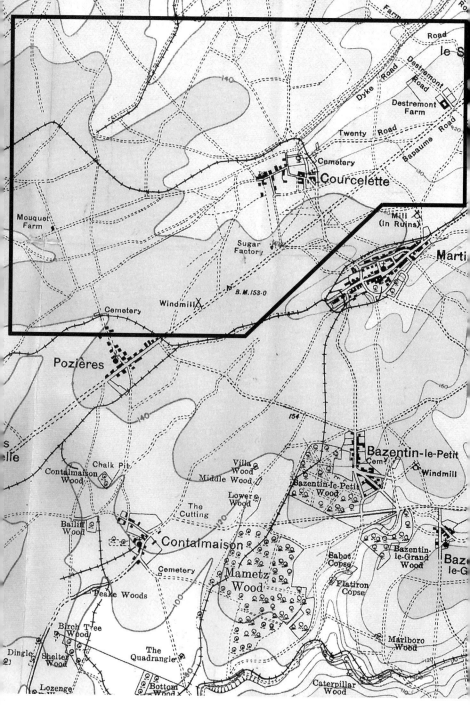

Map 1. The Somme layered. (Official History Map)

Chapter One

CANADA TO COURCELETTE

The Formation of the Canadian Expeditionary Force

When Britain declared war on Germany in August 1914, there was little doubt that the nations of the Empire would follow in their support. Loyalty to King and Empire in Canada was strong and within days of the outbreak of hostilities the Canadian Prime Minister, Sir Robert Borden, called a special wartime session of parliament with the words that, "... we are all agreed; we stand shoulder to shoulder with Britain and the other British Dominions in this quarrel. And that duty we shall not fail to fulfil as the honour of Canada demands."

On the eve of the Great War the only regular military forces in Canada, the Permanent Active Militia, consisted of the Royal Canadian Dragoons, the Lord Strathcona's Horse (both cavalry regiments) and the Royal Canadian Regiment, the only regular infantry battalion. In addition there were various artillery, engineer and support units. In total the Permanent Active Militia numbered a mere 3,000 men. However, in addition there were many other part-time militia units, the Canadian equivalent of the British Territorial Force. These formed thirty-six cavalry and 106 infantry battalions- over 60,000 men.

A plan existed by 1914 to mobilise these men in time of war into an overseas contingent, but the Minister of Militia, Sam Hughes, had other ideas. He sent orders to officers commanding all permanent and non-permanent militia units instructing them to ask for volunteers to form a series of numbered infantry battalions which would be part of a new 'Canadian Expeditionary Force' (CEF).

The volunteers would travel to a new camp at Valcartier, where the Expeditionary Force would assemble, train and be properly organised. From August 1914 thousands of men descended on Valcartier Camp, and although chaos ensued for a time, within a month the camp was made ready into a proper military establishment housing 32,665 Canadian soldiers. From this nucleus the 1st Canadian Division was formed, made up of twelve numbered infantry battalions, along with support units - artillery, engineers and cavalry. Men were issued with specially made tunics, caps bearing a universal bronze maple leaf badge, leather equipment of a very basic design and eventually Canadian Ross Rifles - a weapon which proved unpopular and unreliable in the later history of the CEF. It performed fine on the ranges of Valcartier Camp, but the mud of Flanders and the rigorous

The newly formed Canadian Expeditionary Force (CEF) marches into Valcartier Camp, September 1914.

conditions of trench warfare would eventually secure its downfall.

While the CEF was being assembled at Valcartier Camp, a veritable private army was being raised by a leading Canadian citizen, Captain A. Hamilton Gault. He named his new unit, composed almost entirely of former men of the regular British army, after the daughter of the Governor General of Canada and it therefore became the Princess Patricia's Canadian Light Infantry (PPCLI). When it first paraded the 1,000 men who composed the battalion represented with their former military service every infantry regiment in the British army except one. Needing little training, the PPCLI were speedily dispatched to England, and by December 1914 were in France - the first Canadian infantry battalion to achieve that distinction. Meanwhile the only regular infantry battalion in the Canadian Militia, the Royal Canadian Regiment (RCR), were somewhat ironically sent to Bermuda on Garrison duties just as the PPCLI were on their way to war. Here the RCR relieved the 2nd Lincolnshires who were then released for service in the British Expeditionary Force. The RCR remained here for several months before joining the CEF in France.

By October 1914 the 1st Canadian Division was ready for overseas service, and sailed for England on 3rd October 1914 in a vast flotilla of transport ships - carrying some 31,000 officers and men. It reached Plymouth eleven days later and after disembarking went into further

The Royal Canadian Regiment arrive at Bermuda to relieve 2nd Lincolns. The men were issued with British Khaki Drill uniforms.

Typical CEF recruits in training, late 1914. These men have British Long Lee Enfields while they wait for their Ross Rifles.

training on Salisbury Plain. Here they were to remain until February 1915. The weather during this period was to prove appalling, it being the wettest winter then on record. Camped in tents, the men lived in a sea of mud until huts were eventually erected. By February 1915 orders arrived which would take the 1st Division to France. Commanded by Lieutenant-General E.A.H. Alderson, a regular British officer, the Division landed at St Nazaire on 16th February 1915. In many respects the formation of the Canadian Expeditionary Force had been a marvellous achievement - to raise, train, equip and make a division of volunteers ready for war service in a matter of six months. No other British formation ever matched this record; the first Kitchener's Army division (the 9th) landed in France over three months after the 1st Canadian Division.

Experiences in France and Flanders 1915-16

The units of the 1st Canadian Division were initially attached to battalions of the 4th and 6th British army divisions for instruction purposes in the trenches around Armentieres. From there the division first took over the line at Fleurbaix, and afterwards moved to the Ypres Salient in Belgium. Trenches north-east of Ypres were taken over from British units, and alongside French colonial troops. On the night of 22nd April 1915 the Germans released poison gas against the allied positions in this part of the Salient; here gas was being used for the first time on the Western Front in what became the Second Battle of Ypres. Three weeks of desperate fighting followed around the village of St Julien and the nearby Kitchener's Wood. L/Cpl Fred Fisher won the division's first Victoria Cross on 23rd April 1915, but never knew his fame, being killed the next day. By the close of the fighting the 1st Canadian Division had suffered over 6,000 casualties - some 2,000 of them killed in action or died of wounds.

Meanwhile in Canada a second division was being formed. Further infantry battalions had been sent to England in February 1915 as reinforcements to the 1st Division, but the movement of a second formation was made impossible due to lack of shipping and space to put them in England. The new 2nd Canadian Division differed from the original in respect that the three infantry brigades were organised by area of recruitment, thus giving them a 'local' feel. The 4th Brigade had units from Ontario, the 5th from Quebec and the 6th from Western Canada. The division eventually landed in England in May 1915, just as the Second Battle of Ypres was coming to a conclusion. Based at Shorncliffe, the division was inspected by King George V on 2nd September 1915, proceeding to France two weeks later. They were commanded by Brigadier-General R.E.W. Turner VC, who had won his decoration in the Boer War and had commanded the 3rd Canadian Brigade during Second Ypres. Concentrating at Hazebrouck, the

These Canadians in a communcation trench keep their heads down as they are well within range of German rifles, hand grenades and trench motars. They put on a brave face for the photographer, in spite of the conditions they are having to endure.

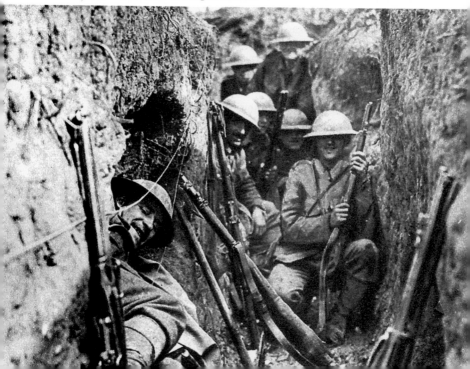

arrival of the 2nd Division meant that a Canadian Corps could now be formed. General Alderson, 1st Division, was appointed to command it, Brigadier-General A.W. Currie taking his place in the 1st Division. The Corps moved entirely to the Ypres Salient where it would remain until the summer of 1916.

Two further actions involving the Canadian Corps took place in the Ypres Salient prior to their move to the Somme in the summer of 1916. The first occurred at St Eloi in April 1916 when the 2nd Division was in action for the first time. The battle revolved around a series of mine craters astride the Ypres-Lille road and between the 4th and 6th April 1916 the division suffered some 1,337 casualties. These losses were made up with further reinforcement drafts from CEF units in England and by this time a third Canadian Division had joined the Corps. This new formation went into battle at Hill 62 in June 1916, when the heaviest bombardment then known to the Canadians was followed by an attack on the positions on both Hill 62 and Mount Sorrel to the south. During the fighting the divisional commander, Major-General Mercer, had been killed and a Brigade commander missing, which weakened the chain of command. The Canadian positions were captured by strong German forces, but a carefully considered counter-attack planned by the new Corps Commander, Sir Julian Byng, pushed the enemy off these low ridges around Ypres on June 12th. Casualties in the Corps had been heavy; in twelve days the losses amounted to 8,430 killed, wounded and missing. However, a fourth Canadian Division had been brought to France in August 1916 and spent its first period of trench service in the line at Ypres. At this stage it was independent of the Canadian Corps, being attached to a British Corps.

Journey To The Somme

The Canadian Corps began to arrive on the Somme in late August 1916. The 1st Division led the move south, and for many the first experience of the area came with the town of Albert. Positioned just behind the British lines on the Somme front, it had been heavily shelled since the outbreak of war but not as badly as Ypres. Approaching the town along the dusty Picardy lanes, the 2nd Bn (Central Ontario) got their first view.

"In the valley below were the ruins of Albert, not all of the homes destroyed; and, provoking voluble comment, the Church of Notre Dame Brebieres, with its 'Hanging Virgin'. The legend surrounding the statue was well-known, nor did its mysticism lose any spiritual qualities in the re-telling. With more hope than

The famous 'Leaning Virgin' in Albert - which all Canadian soldiers saw upon their arrival on the Somme in September 1916.

faith the prophetic utterances, passed along from the Imperial Troops, were repeated: when the Virgin toppled from her precarious perch, the war would end. It is not to be denied that those who found some comfort from the legend hoped longingly for the Virgin's fall in 1916." [1]

The 14th Bn (Royal Montreal Regiment) were in the town soon afterwards and noted,

"... as they passed the famous church crowned by the leaning statue of the Virgin, which hung precariously with outstretched arms, as if to protect and bless the troops beneath." [2]

It was an image of the Somme few veterans were to forget and many thousands sent picture postcards depicting the 'Golden Virgin' home to family and friends. Elsewhere the 15th Bn (48th Highlanders) found,

"... Albert was all but deserted of civilians but troops were plentiful - mud-caked, grey-faced men straight from the line and clean uniformed Canadians." [3]

On the outskirts of Albert was The Brickfields, a large billeting area among an old brick factory. The 2nd Bn found it,

"... an inhospitable area of chalky ground, scantily covered with grass, on the low ridge west of the town. Bare and uninviting at the best of times.

On the Brickfields the men quickly discovered that boxes of Small Arms Ammunition could be built into substantial walls; and when a tarpaulin was thrown over them an adequate hutment was the result. Diligently they applied themselves to the task of creating comfort, their industry accelerated by the downpour which began to drench the place. Huddled within their improvised shelters, they paid little heed to the long-range shelling which was scattered indiscriminately over the area." [4]

About this time 'battle flashes', distinguishing cloth patches, were issued to every man in the CEF. These were in two parts, the lower

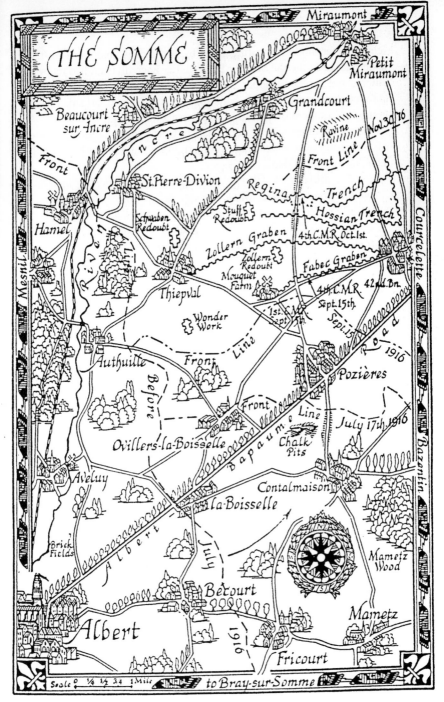

MAP 1 : The Somme front - September 1916.

21

section a rectangle measuring three by two inches, and worn on the upper sleeve of the the Service Dress tunic. Each division had its own colour, and a second upper section of varied shapes and secondary colours distinguished each battalion within its own brigade. At a glance it was therefore possible to discern a man's unit.

Beyond Albert men of the Canadian Corps soon caught a glimpse of the terrain over which they would fight on the Somme battlefield. The 2nd Bn found that,

> *"... forward of Albert the vista was one of sterile, shell-pocked ridges, above which floated the countless observation balloons. The location of these roughly paralleled the windings of the battle-line. The rumble of gunfire was deep and steady, punctuated by the closer, throaty coughs of heavy batteries emplaced on the outskirts of the town. All around were the evidences of what was involved in a great offensive - artillery parks, ammunition dumps, horse lines, watering troughs, stores of gasoline, engineering material, and everywhere, khaki-clad soldiers."* [5]

The Corps was posted to the sector around Pozieres and Mouquet Farm, where Australian troops had been fighting since mid-July. The way up to the line was a tortuous one. The 2nd Bn historian recalled one such journey soon after arriving on the Somme.

> *"At Casualty Corner the climb up the slope of Pozieres Ridge began. Australian guides, tall rangy men in loose-fitting khaki blouses, met the Companies and led them over the sinuous paths that skirted shell holes and throughout the devastation that was once Pozieres village.*
>
> *The front line trench was just beyond the crest. The battalion's right flank rested at a point about 150 yards west of the Windmill. The line continued westerly for about 700 yards, where it met 'Centre Way' - a communication trench - at right angles. From here a new section had been dug diagonally north-west to 'Tom's Cut' which carried the front line forward almost due north. It descended abruptly into a valley, at whose north-western end was Thiepval, a mile and a half away, and rose up the face of another ridge opposite, behind which was Mouquet Farm."* [6]

The 15th Bn found similar conditions.

> *"Pozieres was fantastically obliterated, a scrambled mound of red bricks, bristling timbers and torn fragments of homes, the whole half-buried under the mud sprayed everywhere by the shells."* [7]

Thiepval —

Ancre Valley

Ovillers-la-Boisselle

la Boisselle

Mouquet Farm

Bécourt

Sausage Valley

COURCELETTE

Pozières

Bécourt Wood

Albert-Bapaume Road

Martinpuich

The view is from the Centre Way towards The Windmill.

Here at Pozieres the 1st Canadian Division would participate in the first Canadian engagements of the Battle of the Somme.

The Canadian Scottish at Mouquet Farm

The 16th Bn (Canadian Scottish) was a unit which had fought with distinction in earlier battles of the war, particularly at Second Ypres in April 1915. Commanded by Major Peck, who would win the Victoria Cross later in the war, the battalion was posted to the line on 2nd September 1916, opposite the infamous Mouquet Farm, or 'Mucky Farm' as the troops called it - a large court de ferme, now in ruins, which stood on high ground between Thiepval and Pozieres. Here they relieved the weary Australians who had been battling for possession of the farm for many weeks. The scene was one of utter desolation and carnage.

> *"Bodies were lying everywhere ... some partly buried, others above ground, in various states of mutilation. One body close to me was absolutely naked, covered with wounds."* [8]

Confusion reigned in the line. Major Peck soon lost contact with many of his men, and the truth was that no-one really seemed to know exactly where the front line was. Conditions worsened.

> *"Above ground the dark night, the rain, and the intense enemy shelling combined to demoralise; below ground, in the shelter where the Australian battalion's headquarters and regimental aid post were both stationed, the atmosphere in another way was equally*

This sign painted on the side of a packing case showed the way to Mouquet Farm.

24

depressing. The dug-out, if it could be called by that name, for it was but two large holes, with a dozen or so steps leading down to them, was ill-ventilated, crowded with men sitting on the stairs and lying about on the floor. On entering the place the first whiff of the vitiated atmosphere, heavy with the vapour rising from the damp clothes of the runners and linesmen, who were resting between spells of duty, and the odours from the dressing station, which was separated from headquarters only by a blanket, made any newcomer shiver. The air was so bad that the candles burned with but a faint glimmer. The Australians, lithe, wiry soldiers, full of grit, were utterly exhausted. Information from the front line was almost unobtainable, and what little there was was not particularly helpful." [9]

The battalion found itself holding the longest frontage on record both within brigade and divisional papers. Heavy shelling was combined with small-scale German attacks, but,

"... in a measure this saved the morale of our men, for, however demoralising, the shell fire, directly the sentries called 'they're coming over' all were on their toes." [10]

Shells fell thick and fast, but many failed to explode as one 16th Bn man noted,

"... I never saw so many 'duds', you could hear them hit in great numbers at the rear of the trench. Many came in amongst us and our fellows would coolly lift them out over the parapet." [11]

The men in the front line were in poor shape. One company had had no food or water for three days. Another was being bombarded mercilessly by enfilade fire. Reinforcements were desperately needed, but brigade headquarters refused to allow Major Peck to send up more men. Just past midnight on 5th/6th September an urgent call for troops was received at battalion headquarters, but all Peck could do was send up a runner with a message saying he had no authority to act upon this request. The note never arrived as the runner erroneously ran straight out into No Man's Land and was never seen again. The front line companies hung on, eagerly awaiting news of their fate.

Mouquet Farm 1916.

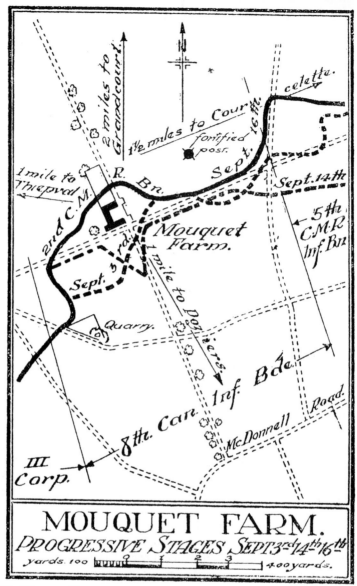

The Mouquet Farm sector - September 1916.

Shelling continued and grew in intensity throughout 6th September. One bomb-block of six men was wiped out by the explosion of a single shell. Seeing this the Germans rushed the position and took it. A counter-attack by the weary 16th Bn secured it back again, but the last of the Lewis gun teams in the area were wiped out. By the afternoon of 6th September a report from the battalion Intelligence Officer made it clear that an insufficient garrison held the line opposite Mouquet Farm, which might threaten the whole position there. In one company alone all that was left was one officer, one warrant officer and twelve men. Brigade headquarters finally relented, and the 16th Battalion was relieved by two other Canadian battalions on 7th September. Later a Canadian Scottish veteran recalled,

> "... taking it all in all, Mouquet Farm was the most nerve-racking, hellish time I ever put in; a lifetime in three days. Even now, after the lapse of these many years, I shudder at the thought of my experiences there." [12]

At Mouquet Farm the Canadian Scottish suffered more casualties than any other engagement of the war, aside from the fighting at Ypres in April 1915. Reflecting the terrible nature of the conditions here at that time, among the wounded were over sixty cases of shell shock.

The 2nd Bn at Pozieres: Leo Clarke VC

After a tour of the trenches on Pozieres Ridge in early September 1916, the 2nd Bn were moved into bivouacs at Sausage Valley near La Boisselle, many men occupying old German dugouts. The weather was warm and dry and, relieved to be out of the line, men set about making their temporary quarters more hospitable. Equally they knew such peace could not last, as by now the whole of the 1st Canadian Division had arrived on the Somme - which meant something more than just daily trench routine was surely in the offing.

On the evening of 8th September Colonel Swift, commanding 2nd Bn, called his company officers together at battalion headquarters to discuss some operation orders which had just been passed down from 1st Brigade. The task before Swift and his men was to capture the last remaining section of German trench on the Pozieres Ridge, a line some 500 yards long running between Pozieres and Martinpuich. The attack would be a forerunner for a much larger operation, whose success depended on the capture of this German trench which dominated the battlefield in this area. The plan would involve an advance in broad daylight, with only a short preliminary bombardment of three minutes duration. During this time the battalion would have to get as close as possible to the German positions, and when the barrage lifted they

Shelling had reduced the Pozieres-Courcelette sector to a wasteland.

would have to make a swift, decisive attack.

Colonel Swift and his men moved up to the British front line via Munster Alley and Peg Trench on the early afternoon of 9th September. Zero Hour had been set for 4.45pm. A new assembly trench was dug before the British lines, and while waiting to go over a party of officers arrived from Brigade headquarters. One of them was Lieutenant Bovill, an official cinematographer, who had been assigned to film the 2nd Bn's attack - the first offensive operation involving Canadian troops on the Somme front. Colonel Swift passed Bovill on to the battalion's Scout Officer who,

> " ... harassed by many duties attendant upon preparations for an attack [and] himself wholly unacquainted with the technique of motion pictures, conducted Bovill to a deep roomy shell-hole between Luxton Trench and the front line. Giving the camera-man curt orders to 'stay there, and not get tangled up in the show', the Scout Officer washed his hands of the matter."[13]

But Bovill soon quit his position and just before Zero managed to crawl forward to the assembly position and film the 2nd Bn going over.

Shells began to drop on the German positions at 4.45 pm, and those in the assembly trench immediately moved forward close to the barrage. The number of 'shorts', shells dropping short of their target, were great and several men were felled by fire from their own guns. As the bombardment lifted,

> " ... along the whole front rose German forage caps. The levelled rifles spat a vicious stream into the Assaulting Wave ... The men dropped into shell-holes, seeking to exchange shots with the Germans, while at the same time worming their way forward on their stomachs. Complicating their difficulties, the enemy artillery laid down a heavy bombardment." [14]

Major A.E. McLaughlin was one of the first officers to fall;

> "There was something particularly poignant about Arthur McLaughlin's death, which befell the following day in [a] Casualty Clearing Station. He was an elderly man, as age is reckoned in the Army. In his native town of Bowmanviller, Ont., he had lived the retiring life of a well-to-do lawyer, interested in promoting the welfare of his community. A gentleman of high intellectual attainment, possessed of a well-stored, cultured mind, and with a genuine charm of manner that reflected the deep sincerity and fineness of a sterling character, he was an appealing figure in the role of Platoon Commander, breasting the fiery hurricane that swept Pozieres Ridge on the afternoon of

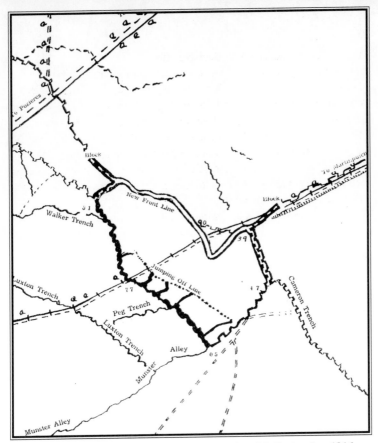

MAP 3: The proposed attack area of the 2nd Bn, 9th September 1916.
TOM GUDMESTAD

9th September 1916... Armed with a cane, he waved his platoon forward, painfully and feebly, as he sank into a shell-hole. The men stumbled on in the teeth of the storm."[15]

The battalion pushed on and into the German trenches, *"...bayoneting the thickly clustered Germans"*. Fierce hand-to-hand followed, and slowly the Germans were pushed out. Some tried to run, but were shot down. The battalion bombers played a particularly important role, and at one point a small group of men, Corporal Leo Clarke among them, set about putting up a bomb block on the left flank to prevent any counter-attacks. Just then a group of twenty Germans, led by two officers, came round the traverse of the trench and attempted to rush the block.

"Corporal Clarke and Pte Soppitt abandoned the block-building operations to the others, and advanced boldly to meet the Germans. The lighter 'egg-bombs' of the enemy

Leo Clarke VC.
TOM GUDMESTAD

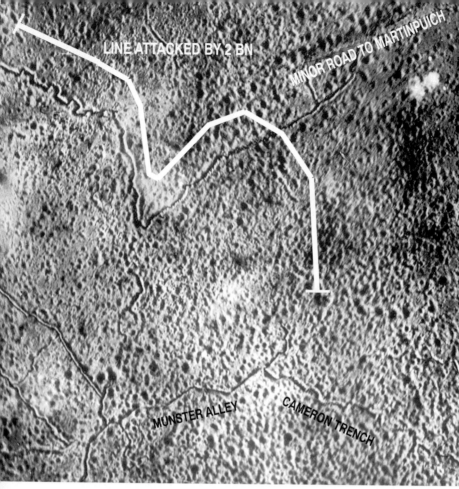

An aerial photograph of the ground over which the 2nd Bn attacked on 9th September 1916 - giving some idea of the conditions here at that time.
ED STORY

out-ranged them, but keeping them at bay Clarke set about erecting a temporary barricade. Again the Germans attacked. The corporal emptied his revolver into them, refilled and emptied it a second time. Every shot counted. Then picking up a German rifle from the trench-floor he fired the undischarged cartridges.

But the enemy were now on him. One of the officers, seizing a rifle, made a lunge at the corporal, wounding him in the knee. Clarke shot him dead. In their sanguinary path up the trench the enemy had left a wake of casualties, yet a few were still capable of putting the corporal out of action. Bleeding profusely, the

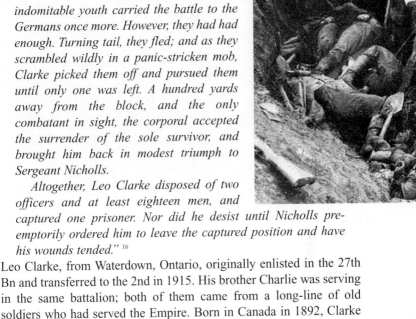

indomitable youth carried the battle to the Germans once more. However, they had had enough. Turning tail, they fled; and as they scrambled wildly in a panic-stricken mob, Clarke picked them off and pursued them until only one was left. A hundred yards away from the block, and the only combatant in sight, the corporal accepted the surrender of the sole survivor, and brought him back in modest triumph to Sergeant Nicholls.

Altogether, Leo Clarke disposed of two officers and at least eighteen men, and captured one prisoner. Nor did he desist until Nicholls pre-emptorily ordered him to leave the captured position and have his wounds tended."* [16]

Leo Clarke, from Waterdown, Ontario, originally enlisted in the 27th Bn and transferred to the 2nd in 1915. His brother Charlie was serving in the same battalion; both of them came from a long-line of old soldiers who had served the Empire. Born in Canada in 1892, Clarke spent his formative years in England and returned to Canada with his parents when he was eleven, and came to live in Winnipeg. On the outbreak of war he was working as a surveyor in northern Canada and served in Flanders before coming down to the Somme. For his bravery that day on Pozieres Ridge he was awarded the Victoria Cross, and promoted Sergeant. Recovering from his wounds quickly, he was soon back with the 2nd Bn. Leo Clarke was the first Canadian to be awarded the supreme medal for gallantry in the Somme Offensive. During operations near Regina Trench Leo Clarke was mortally wounded, dying at a Base Hospital in Le Havre. He was buried in Etretat Churchyard and his grave can be found in the military cemetery there today.

By 5.08 pm the 2nd Bn had captured the position - some twenty-three minutes after going over. Clarke had saved the left flank, and the newly won trench was secure. German dead lay everywhere, and the battalion itself had suffered nearly 200 losses by this time. Now they must hang on to what they had gained, under fierce enfilade fire from Martinpuich. Bombing attacks resumed on the left flank where Clarke had held out. Punishment continued with a heavy German bombardment, but the battalion clung on until the afternoon of 10th September, when Colonel Swift and his men were relieved by the 19th

A contemporary illustration of Leo Clarke winning his VC.

Bn. The operation had cost them dear: six officers and 123 other ranks killed in action, six officers and 210 other ranks wounded. The '9th of the 9th' passed into battalion history as a costly, but glorious day, and as the tired survivors marched back towards billets in Albert they were met with cheers from other 1st Division men who lined the route, crying, 'Good Old Second!'.

With the clearance of this trench on the Pozieres Ridge the 2nd Bn had opened the way for a further advance. Plans were now made for the next objective – Courcelette.

Chapter Notes

1. Murray, W.W. The History of the 2nd Canadian Battalion (Eastern Ontario Regiment) Canadian Expeditionary Force in the Great War p.113.
2. Featherstonhaugh, R.C. The Royal Montreal Regiment, 14th Battalion C.E.F. 1914-1925 (Gazette Printing Co. 1927) p.108.
3. Beattie, K. 48th Highlanders of Canada 1891-1928 (Southam Press Ltd 1932) p. 161.
4. Murray op cit p.113-114.
5. ibid. p.113.
6. ibid. p.115-116.
7. Beattie op cit. p.162.
8. Urquart, H.M. The History of the 16th Battalion (The Canadian Scottish) C.E.F. In The Great War 1914-1919 (McMillan Coy of Canada 1932) Chap.XIII9. ibid. p.
10. ibid. p.
11. ibid. p.
2512. ibid. p.
13. Murray op cit. p.123.
14. ibid. p.125.
15. ibid.
16. ibid. p.126-127.

Chapter Two

THE CAPTURE OF COURCELETTE
15 SEPTEMBER 1916

The Canadian Corps assembled for the Battle of Flers-Courcelette; another phase in the continuation of the Battle of the Somme and an advance across a wide front from Courcelette on the left, to Flers and as far as Leuze Wood near Combles on the right. Aside from the Canadians, a further nine British divisions would leave their trenches at Zero Hour on 15th September 1916. Accompanying them for the

Over The Top! Canadian soldiers attack Courcelette.

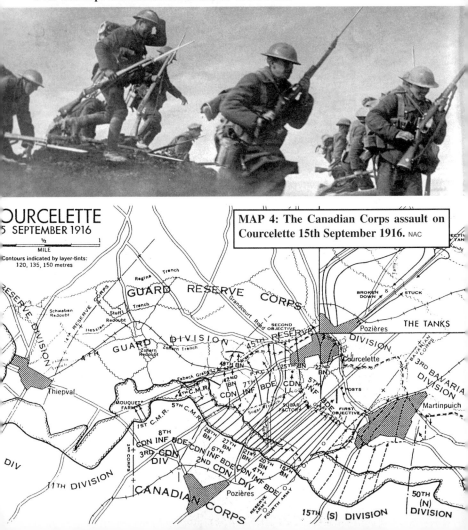

MAP 4: The Canadian Corps assault on Courcelette 15th September 1916. NAC

first time in the history of warfare were tanks - so-called 'Landships' of the Heavy Section Machine Gun Corps. Developed from prototypes based on agricultural tractors, and built by Fosters of Lincoln, these new machines came in two forms. The 'Male' was armed with two six-pounder naval guns; each in a turret or sponson either side of the tank. The 'Female' version had similar sponsons, but these carried Vickers machine-guns. At Courcelette one tank section was attached to the Canadian Corps. In examining what happened in the day's fighting at Courcelette I will look at the battalions and units on an individual basis, starting with the first attack in the morning of 15th September and moving on to the fighting later in the day.

18th and 20th Bns

The 18th (Western Ontario) and 20th (Central Ontario) Bns were given the right hand flank joining the British lines south-east of Pozieres. Both had a battalion frontage of around 250 yards, with Lieutenant-Colonel Rogers' 20th Bn attacking on the left astride the Albert-Bapaume road, and Lieutenant-Colonel Milligan's 18th Bn on the far right. Some 1,200 yards before them across No Man's Land, and the German front line, lay the 4th Brigade objective - Candy Trench, a strong German position south of the Sugar Factory which ran towards Martinpuich. Behind them in the attack were elements of the 19th Bn who would act as mopping up troops as the main waves moved forward.

On the night of 14th September men of the 20th Bn were,

> *"... making final arrangements for the great event of the morrow, when for the first time we would leave the cover of the trenches to advance under a shower of shells and bullets, and engage the enemy hand to hand. Our preparations were made with infinite care. Newcomers and originals, with every confidence in themselves, were determined to establish a reputation for the 20th Battalion."* [1]

The bombardment of the German forward positions and Candy Trench was by then reaching a crescendo until 4am, when the barrage ceased and the hours leading up to Zero crept slowly onwards. At this point the Germans made an unexpected move against the Canadian lines. Major F. Davey recalled,

> *"... a determined attack by a strong enemy bombing party was made upon the right sector of the 4th Brigade front. A portion of the attacking party had actually reached our trenches at the time the attack started. It was overcome by vigorous bombing and*

rifle fire. A bombing officer in the disputed section, Lieutenant Hugh H. Sykes, 18th Battalion, promptly organised his defence and effectively maintained his position. Lieutenant Gidley, of the 19th Battalion, and parties of bombers from that unit and the 20th Battalion also took part, and frustrated what might have developed into a formidable attack had the initial attempt been successful. The enemy's preparations for this attack eventually told against him, for the strong force he placed in his front trenches to exploit any initial success suffered heavily as our barrage came down upon it." [2]

Veterans of Courcelette: RSM Collett (seated centre) of the 20th Bn was awarded the MC for his bravery on 15th September 1916.

For a moment it seemed that the advance might have been checked before it began, but Lieutenants Sykes and Gidley had saved the position. The fire-fight continued until after Zero Hour, as the rest of 4th Brigade moved forward.

Zero Hour itself finally came at 6.20am, when the men of the 18th and 20th Bns advanced on Candy Trench. As they moved across No Man's Land very little small arms fire was coming from the German positions, and their front line was entered and occupied within fifteen minutes. The Canadians then bombed their way through the bays and traverses towards the next objective. On the 18th Bn front Major S.M. Loghrin took the surrender of a party of Germans until one threw a concealed Stick Grenade at him, instantly killing Loghrin. Outraged, the Major's comrades showed no mercy as the Germans were dealt with at the point of the bayonet. Despite this both battalions pushed on and Candy Trench was soon taken, again with little resistance.

From here Captain Heron MC, of the 20th Bn, who was in some of the most forward positions, pushed on a further 800 yards along the Albert-Bapaume road to Gun Pit Trench in an unplanned and impromptu attack. His daring party bombed out several dugouts, and returned to Candy Trench with two prisoners and two captured machine-guns. Heron reported to Lieutenant-Colonel Rogers that Gun Pit Trench was lightly held and so the men of the 4th Brigade moved

A German Minenwerfer crew captured by men of the 20th Bn.
ED STOREY

forward again and by 10am the trench was in Canadian hands; over fifty prisoners and various weapons being taken in the advance. Here an outpost line was set up opposite the nearby sunken road leading from the Courcelette crossroads on the Albert-Bapaume road to Martinpuich and the men dug in - where they remained until relief on the 17th September. On the way out to billets in Albert the two battalions paused in Sausage Valley near La Boisselle to bury some of their dead. Total casualties for the 20th Bn alone had been ten officers and 279 men.

21st Bn

On the morning of 15th September, the men of 21st (Eastern Ontario) Bn were assembling in positions just beyond the Pozieres Windmill, north of the Albert-Bapaume road. Three companies were in the front line , with one in reserve to follow up the attack. Before them was the main objective here - Courcelette Sugar Factory. At Zero Hour the preliminary bombardment lifted to a hundred yards beyond the German front line and the 21st Bn advanced, covered by machine-gun fire from the Canadian Machine Gun Corps. Lance Cattermole was a private in the 21st Bn that day and left a detailed and harrowing account of the part played by his battalion. Cattermole had emigrated to Canada before the Great War to farm, and had joined the 76th

Battalion under age in 1915. He had transferred to the 21st Bn with a draft from England in mid-1916, and had previously served in the Ypres Salient before coming down to the Somme.

Lance Cattermole.

"We arrived at our jumping-off trench with none too much time to spare. This was probably intentional so that we did not have too long to wait before going over. We dropped into the trench beside those who were holding it, and regained our breath from our tiring walk. We had marched overland in the darkness and heavy ground mist from Happy Valley, on the SE side of the main road where we had been in reserve in shallow, old German dugouts.

My platoon was in the third and last wave in the advance (the waves were twenty yards apart). We crawled over the top of the parapet and lined up on a broad, white tape, just discernible in the growing light, immediately in front of the trench and behind the first two waves which were already in position. It was almost Zero Hour. I looked at my wrist watch and saw we had about three minutes to go. I never heard our officers' whistles to signal the advance, and I don't suppose they heard them either because

Canadians testing a Vickers machine-gun, September 1916. The Vickers was the standard medium machine-gun for British and Empire troops.

'A sheet of flame ... belching fire and smoke' - Canadian artillery smashes the positions opposite Lance Cattermole's 21st Bn. (NAC)

of the terrific crash with which the creeping barrage opened up, exactly at 6.20am.

The air over our heads was suddenly filled with the soughing and sighing, whining and screaming of thousands of shells of all calibres, making it impossible to hear anything. We stood up and I looked around behind me; as far as the eye could see, from left to right, there was a sheet of flame from the hundreds of guns lined up, almost wheel to wheel, belching fire and smoke. It was an awe-inspiring sight.

We started our advance, but I had only taken three paces when an enemy shell fell exactly in front of me. All I saw was a great fountain of loose earth, of which I received a mouthfull, and I was flung on my back. I believe it was only a second or two before I struggled to my feet, thinking I was blown to bits! I felt myself all over, and to my amazement I had no injuries whatsoever; I was simply winded. The shell must have been a dud. At this I started to laugh, which I presume was a sign of nervous relief that I was not hit, and I continued my walk forward.

An added noise made me look upwards and, through a break in the swirling morning mist, I saw one of our spotter planes, the wings golden in the rays of the rising sun against a blue sky, showing the red, white and blue roundels of the RFC [Royal Flying Corps]. This gave me a cheerful feeling, and one, too, of a thrilling excitement. I felt that this was a terrific 'show' put on for my benefit, and that I was an actor taking part in an epic film, both feelings at the same time- it was most extraordinary!

I quickened my pace to make up for the time I had lost, when suddenly, on my right, someone shouted: 'Cattie, don't go so fast!'. It was a young lad whom I recognised as being in my platoon in my original battalion before being drafted, with others, to the 21st Battalion in France. I ran over to him and asked him what the matter was. He said, 'Don't go so fast. We

don't know what's in front of us and we can't see.' It is true there
was a wall of mist and smoke in front. I looked down, and there
in the shell holes were five of his friends, all youngsters, all of
whom I knew but had not seen for weeks as we had been split up
during our transfer. They were not afraid - just a little
bewildered, a little unsure, a little lost and only in need of a lead.
They had known me as a Corporal in our old battalion, and I
presume the feeling still existed with them that I was an NCO,
and I like to think they looked to me again. I just shouted, 'Come
on chaps! We must push on!' and I was glad to see they all moved
after me, and we kept going.

It was then that I spotted John Robb[4]. *He was on his knees,*
sitting back on his heels with his arms hanging loosely at his
sides. His helmet was off and his face turn to the sky. There was
on his face a look of the most joyous astonishment. I foolishly,
without realising he had been hit, shouted out, 'Come on, Robb!
What's wrong?' But as I moved round in front of him to his other
side, I saw the blood gushing from his neck where he had
obviously been hit in the jugular. I knew that he was finished,
and in any case we were not allowed to stop to succour
companions in an advance, so there was nothing I could do. I am
not a religious sort of chap. I would find it difficult to write down
what I believe in, and I have mixed ideas about the hereafter; but
I would give a lot to know what that young soldier saw in the sky
as his life blood ebbed away."

The 21st Bn pushed on into the trenches before the Sugar Factory and
Lance Cattermole and his young comrades were now faced with
Germans holding up their hands.

"Suddenly we came upon an enemy trench to our left. In
keeping with our 'no prisoners' order, in view of the past German
treachery, this trench was being mopped up and the occupants
eliminated. The trench was already half-full of dead enemy and
here and there little columns of steam rose in the cool, morning
air, either from the hot blood let or from the urine I understand
is released on the death of any human body. Two Canadians
stood over the trench, one on the parapet and the other on the
parados, and they exterminated the Germans as they came out of
their dugouts.

One young German, scruffy, bareheaded, cropped hair and
wearing steel-rimmed spectacles, ran, screaming with fear,
dodging in and out amongst us to avoid being shot, crying out

A German illustration of the Courcelette Sugar Factory. <small>KLAUS SPATH</small>

'Nein! Nein!'. He pulled out from his breast pocket a handful of photographs and tried to show them to us (I suppose they were of his wife and children) in an effort to gain our sympathy. It was all of no avail. As the bullets smacked into him he fell to the ground motionless, the pathetic little photographs fluttering down to the earth around him."

The battlefield of any war is a place where reason is lost, and men die terribly. Such scenes as this were not unique in the Somme battle, nor on any other part of the Western Front. But episodes such as these often played on the minds of men in the post-war years, men who in civilian life had probably never even kicked a dog. For Lance Cattermole this was to become one of the enduring memories of his front line service, and one he would rarely share with others in his own lifetime. The full story of what happened at Courcelette first appeared in print after his death, when it was published in *Stand To!*, the journal of the Western Front Association.

To continue his story, Cattermole and his comrades were now on the site of the Sugar Factory which was *"... now nothing but a mass of crushed masonry."* From here they pushed on and came across one of their officers.

"Our company commander, his right arm in a sling and looking very pale, stood on a small knoll looking over towards the village of Courcelette to out left front. Evidently he had got to close quarters in taking the German position. Captain Miller was a big man, very silent, almost monosyllabic. The only emotion he seemed to show was a gentle, half smile, and when he spoke you could hardly hear him. When there was the slightest breeze his commands on parade were lost. But he was brave as

Canadians digging in near Courcelette, September 1916. Around them are the bodies of their dead comrades

a lion, and already wore the ribbon of the Military Cross for his work at St Eloi craters some five months earlier. When we were in the Ypres Salient ... he never missed a night, walking and crawling over No Man's Land reconnoitring, always bringing back a snippet of the German wire to show he had been there [5].

As I was walking with a short fellow on my left and a tall lad named Kelly on my right, a 'Jack Johnson' [German shell] landed over to our left with a terrific roar. A piece of shell casing flew past the heads of us smaller chaps hitting Kelly in the shoulder; he let out a yell. As the position had been taken we were able to do what we could for him. We eased off his equipment and I took a clasp knife, which I carried in my right leg puttee like a skean dhu ... and cut the sleeve of his jacket up to the shoulder so as to get at the wound. The piece of shell casing was about an inch thick and a couple of inches square, half buried in the deltoid muscle. It was very hot, but I gradually eased it out and dropped it on the ground. I had already got his field dressing out and undone it, and then I said, 'Kelly, this is going to hurt' and poured a liberal dose of iodine from the phial supplied, as a precaution against tetanus. He went very white, but took it splendidly. I applied the dressing and we put him on

The remains of the Sugar Refinery, 15th September 1916. NAC

the road back down a communication trench to the first advanced dressing post, and so to Blighty where I saw him many months later.

A group of about twenty prisoners were now filed out of the ruins of the sugar refinery and put to work digging a trench a little north of us, I presume for us to man in case of a counter-attack. Two Germans tried to make a run for it. One was brought down when he had only taken a few paces, but the other a big, smart NCO, made a zig-zag course towards the German lines, running very fast; but one of the guards picked him off before he had got thirty yards. His hands went up and he pitched forward on his face and lay still. However, this work of trench-digging was soon given up and the prisoners sent to the rear, I suppose through a change of plan.

About twenty of us who had been in the third wave were now collected together and led forward to the east of the refinery by a young officer whom I did not know, evidently from another platoon. Crossing Candy Trench to get there, I saw two of our poor fellows lying half-buried at the bottom of the trench, their torsos covered by an earth fall from a shell exploding there as they were passing. One body was inert but the other was still quivering, the result of concussion. I never knew whether the lad got out alive. I also saw the smart German NCO who had made a break for it lying on the ground with others, already turning yellow. We were led into a network of communication trenches to the east of the refinery where we stayed all night, squatting in the trenches and dozing when we could. I suppose we ate our iron rations when we felt hungry, but I cannot recall doing this.

Some time in the night we were woken by the young officer in charge of us and told we had to go over the top again to occupy the Sunken Road to our east, which joined the Albert-Bapaume road to the village of Courcelette. Duly, at 6.00am [September 16th] his whistle sounded and we jumped off and went forward. Fortunately this time we had only machine-guns

The Sunken Lane at Courcelette. NAC

firing against us and they were playing them rather high. We small fellows scored, but they were picking off the taller chaps who went down one after the other. One poor chap got five bullets in him. The day before, this same fellow had heard that his brother had been killed, and when he met a German in the advance he went berserk and repeatedly bayoneted him in revenge.

Eventually we dropped down into Sugar Trench and filed into the Sunken Road. We found this was free of the enemy. The road was deserted except for the corpse of an Imperial [British soldier] *lying on his back, his head downhill and his legs splayed out. There was no trace of any wound. How or when he got there I had no idea, because the Canadian Corps now held the sector*[16]. *Strangely, the seam of his trousers crutch was split up and his private parts were displayed. I thought it unkind of the Fates to show a brave warrior so bizarrely exposed.*

As we went further in, however, we found a poor little German hiding in one of the funk holes; he had been hit in the head. One eye bounced about on a cord below his chin and the other socket was empty. The two Canadians who found him could not have been more tender in their ministrations to him and he was eventually got away down the line.

We spread out along the section of the road we were to hold and manned the east brink, which was about 8 to 10 feet high along this stretch. The officer said we must be prepared for a counter-attack. It was still extremely misty out there on the flat land to the east towards Le Sars, and we were instructed to be on the alert. Suddenly the officer ordered 'Rapid fire!'. We obeyed orders, firing into the mist where evidently he had seen movement. Our action probably prevented an attack developing. Possibly the attack went in further down the road towards Courcelette, now in the hands of the 22nd Battalion, which was continually being counter-attacked. After a few minutes he called 'Cease fire!' To my surprise, I found that my rifle was so hot I couldn't touch the barrel.

The morning was wearing on, when unexpectedly a group of Germans appeared round a bend in the road, coming from the direction of the village. They were a band of about five with various wounds, one making a crutch of his rifle, badly wounded in one leg. They were shepherded by a young German who could not have been more than seventeen, with an enormous grey helmet on his head but without any equipment. He was waving a piece of wood to which was attached a home-made Red Cross flag, a piece of white sheeting with the Red Cross obviously dabbed in blood. He was jiggling it up and down, looking over it towards the German lines. Having heard of the various dirty tricks the Germans had carried out under the Red Cross, I dashed up and tried to pull his arms down. 'It's all right, Cattie!' shouted our Corporal, 'He's trying to show his fellows that it's only wounded passing, and I think it's all right'. So we let them go forward up to the Albert-Bapaume road and so back to our lines as wounded prisoners.

Shortly after this I was standing in the road and looking back towards the Sugar Refinery, when I saw a Canadian officer, bare-headed, with a triangular blue scarf tied round his head over his eyes, and hanging down in front of his face, giving the appearance of a bandit on the films. He was dragging himself along the ground and as he could not see, he dropped into the next shell hole. Then he pulled himself out of that and dropped into the next one, and I did not see him again. When our own platoon Corporal came to visit us I told him of this happening, and he said 'Well, he must be one of ours. I will go and have a look for him.' I learned later that he found the officer and pulled him to safety, receiving a sniper's bullet in his buttocks for his gallantry. Obviously the blinded officer had had no idea where he was, and was in fact travelling in the wrong direction. This brave young Corporal, who already wore the MM [Military Medal], recovered from his wound only to have a foot blown off later.

Presently our platoon Sergeant came forward from the main group round the refinery to see how we were getting on. He stood

Canadian wounded being evacuated from the Courcelette battlefield, 15th September 1916. NAC

*up as high as he could in the road and kept looking to the rear,
saying that they had promised the cavalry would would come
and break through if we had taken the position. No cavalry
appeared! No counter-attack developed on our particular
section of the Sunken road either, but there was much activity
going on lower down and round the village. Eventually darkness
came on and we were told we would be relieved at midnight. This
proved true, and our relief filed into the road; we were led out by
a guide, back through Sugar Trench. We found this full of
wounded and one poor Sergeant, lying back against the wall of
the trench, wounded in the leg, said: 'Mind my bloody foot!'
which was terribly difficult to avoid on getting into the trench.
He groaned as I unavoidably touched his foot.*

*We were soon out of the trench to make faster time overland,
once we had got clear of the Sunken Road and its attendant Very
Lights. It now came on to rain slightly which we found refreshing
after the sweating of the day, and we trudged on with the rain
coming into our faces."*

There had been no cavalry, but the 21st Bn's advance had been wholly
successful. However, the cost was soon apparent, as Lance Cattermole
soon found out.

*"Eventually we reached Happy Valley again and we answered
our names at a roll call. There were only about twelve of us left
out of the twenty who had gone forward to occupy the Sunken
Road."*

The battalion cooks dished out a double ration of rum to the survivors
and they slept like babies in some old German funk holes. For Lance
Cattermole, Courcelette was his first and last major action on the
Western Front. Under age, his mother wrote to the Canadian Militia
who removed him from the front line and sent him to a CEF Depot unit
at Seaford Camp in Sussex. Here he ended the war [7].

31st Bn

The 31st (Alberta) Bn were on the left flank of the advance on
Courcelette, near the leading waves of the 27th and 28th Bns who were
astride the Pozieres-Courcelette road. Ahead, across No Man's Land,
was the 6th Brigade objective of Sugar Trench on the left, and Taffy
Trench directly before them. These positions guarded the access to the
village and on the right, the Sugar Factory. The 31st Bn's role was
primarily in mopping-up the ground taken by the leading battalions. In
doing so it inevitably meant that the battalion would be widely

scattered across the battlefield during the attack.

Pte Donald Fraser was serving with the 31st Bn on this day, and like Lance Cattermole left a superb account of his war service[8]. He recalled the initial advance,

> "As Zero Hour approached I glanced round looking for signs to charge. The signal came like a bolt from the blue. Right on the second the barrage opened with a roar that seemed to split the heavens... I was up and over in a trice, running into shell holes, down and up for about twenty yards, until I found that if I continued this procedure and rate, loaded up as I was, I would be exhausted before I could get to grips with Fritz.
>
> It was at this juncture that instinct told me to avoid the shell holes and move along the edges. I raised my head for the first time and looked at the Hun trench, and to my astonishment, saw Heiny after Heiny ranging along the line, up on the firing step, blazing away wildly into us, to all appearances unmolested. Seriousness and grim determination took possession of me as I stared hard and menacing at those death-dealing rifles. Strange to say they all seemed to be pointing at me ... My wits sharpened when it burnt deeply into me that death was in the offing. At this stage an everchanging panorama of events passed quickly before my gaze, and my mind was vividly impressed. The air was seething with shells. Immediately above, the atmosphere was cracking with a myriad of machine-gun bullets, startling and disconcerting in the extreme. Bullets from enemy rifles were whistling and swishing around my ears in hundreds, that to this day I cannot understand how anyone could have crossed the inferno alive."

But cross it alive they did. Fraser and his comrades in the 31st Bn were now moving close to the German lines when another apparition arrived on the battlefield. These were a number of tanks attached to the Canadian Corps, being used for the first time.

> "Lying low in the shell hole contemplating events...a strange and curious sight appeared. Away to my left rear, a huge gray object reared itself into view, and slowly, very slowly, it crawled

Pte Donald Fraser.

CHURCH

RUINS OF
COURCELETTE

SUNKEN LANE

RED CHATEAU

THE QUARRY

N

Courcelette from the air, September 1916. NAC

along like a gigantic toad, feeling its way across the shell-stricken field. It was a tank, the 'Creme de Menthe', *the latest invention of destruction and the first of its kind to be employed in the Great War. I watched it coming towards our direction. How painfully slow it travelled. Down and up the shell holes it clambered, a weird, ungainly monster, moving relentlessly forward. Suddenly men from the ground looked up, rose as if from the dead, and running from the flanks to behind it, followed in the rear as if to be in on the kill. The last I saw of it, it was*

47

wending its way to the Sugar Refinery. It crossed Fritz's trenches, a few yards from me, with hardly a jolt."

Soon after Fraser and his comrades reached the German line before the Sugar Refinery,

"... when I jumped into the trench, the sight I beheld, for sheer bloodiness and murder, baffles description. Apparently our artillery had sent over a last minute shrapnel barrage, for the Huns were terribly mangled about the head and shoulders which, coupled with our sniping, completely wiped out every Heiny in the bays in front of us. Everyone of them was either dead or dying and the trench literally was running blood. As each bay contained three to five men, it required no imagination to picture the carnage."

The battalion was doing well, and some platoons on the left had reached the outskirts of Courcelette itself. Fraser and his men were close on the Sugar Factory, and the positions so far captured were consolidated as the PPCLI and 42nd Bn passed through elements of the 31st Bn, thus continuing the advance. Orders were eventually received to pull back to the old front line as the battle raged on. Here they spent the night of the 15th September before moving further back. Out of the 722 men who went into the attack that morning, only 318 were left to answer the roll call.

The Tanks at Courcelette

Fraser was only one of many Canadians who witnessed the advance of the tanks at Courcelette. The Heavy Section of the Machine Gun Corps had been formed some months before when a tank finally suitable for use in the conditions that prevailed on the Western Front was developed. This was the Mark I, and was crewed by an officer and seven men. The driver was a Sergeant from the Army Service Corps, but the rest of the crew were all Machine Gun Corps men. Six tanks from No 1 Section of C Company Heavy Section were allocated to the Canadian Corps for the attack on Courcelette, commanded by Captain A.M. Inglis, a regular army officer formerly of the Gloucestershire Regiment.

A Mk I female tank, as used by C Company HB MGC at Courcelette.

Captain A.M. Inglis, photographed at Cambrai in November 1917.

Tank C.5, commanded by Captain Inglis himself, was attached to the 4th Brigade for the attack on the Sugar Refinery. Inglis had moved the tank up from Albert on the night before to an Advanced Dressing Station south of Pozieres where the vehicle refuelled. From here the tank made its way up to the Pozieres Windmill, which it reached by 2am. Inglis and his crew waited until Zero Hour, while the shells crashed around them. The tank was hit and one of the tail wheels used for steering was blown off. However, Inglis later wrote,

" ... *At Zero (6.20am) we commenced our advance and made for the Sugar Factory, which was my objective. Soon after crossing our front line trench a group of about 50 Germans came up towards the tank to surrender. Our infantry was well in advance of the tank, and were in the Sugar Factory by the time I arrived; but I was able to make use of my Hotchkiss Guns. I skirted the southern and eastern side of the factory and went up to the trench where our infantry were consolidating. Having found an officer who informed me that the position had been made good, I commenced my return journey, and laid out about 400 yards telephone wire which I carried on the tail of the tank ... Before reaching the Windmill the wire drum was smashed in by a shell. I eventually reached a point on the Pozieres-Albert road 300 yards from Camp, when the track came completely off.*"[9]

The ASC driver managed to bump the monster back to camp and Inglis and his crew returned without injury and having assisted greatly in the advance on the Sugar Factory.

During this action they had been joined by 2/Lt J. Allen's tank, C.6, which, he later reported, had

> "... moved off towards our then front line. Between this line
> and the German front line we were heavily shelled by the enemy
> artillery. Several parties of the enemy were engaged by us and
> finished off by our infantry. The course continued in the direction
> of Courcelette which however we did not enter but turned in
> direction of the Sugar Factory. As the latter positions had by this
> time been consolidated we returned to camp for repair."[10]

Other tanks in No 1 Section had been less fortunate. C.1 under
Lieutenant A.J.C. Wheeler had it's steering wheels damaged by shell
fire, and in the initial stages of the advance the tank bellied and could
not be moved. The crew attempted to dig it out, but by 10.45am the
shelling had become so heavy the task was impossible and Wheeler
abandoned the vehicle, leading his crew back on foot. Thus was the
fate of the other tanks attached to the Canadian Corps at Courcelette.
C.4 shed a track and was immobilised. The steering on C.2 packed up
just beyond Pozieres, and the tank slipped sideways into a
communication trench. Work to recover it continued until 8 pm, but
eventually the crew gave up. C.3 also suffered from steering problems,
but carried on until it ditched in a large shell hole filled with tree
trunks; the engine seized up and it was abandoned. The first use of
tanks in the Great War had not entirely been a tale of dash and glory -
more a catalogue of mechanical faults and bad luck.

The Attack Continued: 42nd Bn

To exploit any potential successes at Courcelette Julian Byng,
commanding the Canadian Corps, had kept back a large body of troops
in reserve around Albert. The advance of the morning on Candy
Trench, Sugar Trench and the Sugar Factory had been so complete that
these reserves could now be brought up to continue the battle.
Courcelette village itself, Fabeck and Zollern Graben - main German
trench lines - still eluded the Canadians.

The 42nd Bn, Black Watch of Canada, a kilted regiment of great
distinction, was part of 7th Brigade, 3rd (Canadian) Division. On the
morning of 15th September it was encamped with other units in the
Brigade around the Brickfields at Albert. At 9am that morning, as the
2nd Division was fighting at Courcelette, a battalion divine service
was being held at the Brickfields when orders demanding a move up to
the front line were received. Some 750 men of the 42nd Bn marched
out of camp, and by 11am were at the designated Brigade assembly
positions near Usna Hill at La Boisselle.

Courcelette Sugar Factory.

Scale:- about 50yds = 1 inch
(Sketch from an Aeroplane
Photograph & is distorted.)

Coordinates agree with
1:5000 map. (Trench)

MAP 5: An intelligence
plan of the extensive area
covered by the Sugar
Factory issued to Inglis
and his men.

49
51
48
Uncemented
Cemented
60
Ponds
A
A

Beet
Pits (VATS)

Chimney
Limekiln
Wash Pit
Boilers
Well Tanks
Factory C
B
New Beet Pit
Cemented
B

87
To Courcelette
To Bapaume

Cellars

Section on A.A.   VATS AND TRENCH.
6yds 8yds 6yds

Section on B.B.
NEW PIT
8yds 2yds

15yds
5yds
Section on C.C.
TANKS.

Canadian Corps Intelligence
Sept. 15th 1916.

The Sugar Factory, Courcelette.
TOM GUDMESTAD

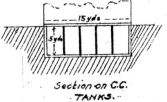

Information coming into Brigade headquarters about the conduct of the fighting at Courcelette was contradictory, but it was clear that the initial advances had been successful and a further attack would be needed. No detailed instructions arrived, but it was passed down that an operation would be initiated within the next few hours, involving the 42nd Bn on the left and PPCLI on the right. They would pass through the men already opposite Courcelette and advance on Fabeck Graben, a long German trench running from Mouquet Farm to Courcelette. A sunken lane, one of several in the area and known as MacDonnell Road, lying roughly parallel with Fabeck Graben, but about 600 yards short of this objective, would be the first obstacle known to be in German hands. From here they would push on to Fabeck Graben itself.

Lieutenant-Colonel Cantlie, commanding 42nd Bn, assembled his officers and explained the problems that confronted them,

"... four and a half hours only were available to march five miles over difficult country devoid of land marks, through enemy barrages, to deploy for the attack in broad daylight in a captured and partly obliterated German trench, the whereabouts of which was not known except from the map, to the Battalion Commanders, and to launch the attack on a two Battalion front at 6pm" [11]

The battalion moved up through this terrain, the rubble of Pozieres village, at 4.30pm and cut onto the ground leading to Sugar Trench, which would be the jumping off position mentioned by Lieutenant-Colonel Cantlie. Shells were dropping around them almost continuously, but the Highlanders advanced in extended order and "... this movement on the slope outside Pozieres was carried out with almost parade ground precision notwithstanding a number of casualties"[12]. Lieutenant-Colonel Cantlie himself was struck by a piece of shell fragment, which painfully bruised his forearm, but he pushed on with his men.

Lt-Col G.S. Cantlie DSO. TOM GUDMESTAD

Despite the conditions, Sugar Trench was reached by 5.45pm and the battalion jumped off almost at once at 6pm, just giving them time to pause for breath before moving on. The Highlanders headed for MacDonnell Road, following a bombardment laid down before them, which lifted from this position at 6.15pm to

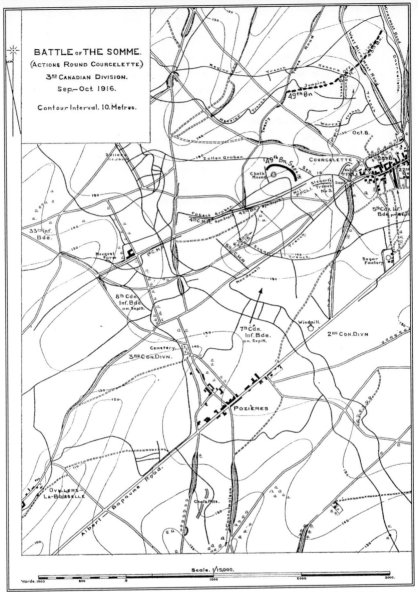

MAP 6: The area of operations of 3rd (Canadian) Division 15th-16th September 1916. TOM GUDMESTAD

Fabeck Graben itself. No resistance of any consequence was encountered in the first objective, which was captured only minutes after the protective fire had moved on. After reorganising in the sunken lane, the attack was resumed at 6.25pm, and with shells still falling thick and heavy on Fabeck Graben the 42nd Bn advanced across 600 yards of rising ground with the heavily manned German position on the crest before them.

Fire was now brought down on the attacking Highlanders, with several officers and men becoming casualties almost immediately on leaving the cover of the sunken road. However, the two leading companies entered Fabeck Graben with a rush. It was found that the bombardment,

> "... had been particularly effective and had completely demoralised the garrison, many of whom could be seen running from the trench." [13]

The Highlanders now dug in, and made contact with the PPCLI on the right who were having a much more difficult time. Behind those in Fabeck Graben, the other two companies of the 42nd Bn were consolidating in another sunken road, known as Mouquet Road on trench maps, which now came under heavy fire from German artillery. At this point the officer in command at Mouquet Road, Captain C. Blair Wilson, was killed and a junior Lieutenant took over. However, it had been a successful operation for the 42nd Bn. Many prisoners were taken in Fabeck Graben, along with two trench mortars and several machine-guns. The Black Watch spent the night in these forward positions, as a drizzle slowly settled in on the battlefield.

Princess Patricia's Canadian Light Infantry

The Princess Patricia's Canadian Light Infantry (PPCLI) had seen more front line service than any other unit in the CEF by mid-1916. Few of the originals were left at the time of the Somme, but the battalion still retained something of an 'elite' status within the Canadian Corps. Flanders had worn the battalion down, and they saw the move to Picardy as a *'breath of fresh air'*, but such illusions were soon shattered when beyond Albert they found

> "... a slimy sea of shell-holes where no green thing remained" [14].

On the morning of 15th September the PPCLI were still under

Lieut.-Colonel R T

bivouacs at the Brickfields along with the 42nd Bn and other units of 7th Brigade. They were awoken at 6.20am by the bombardment at Courcelette, and the command to *'Stand To'* and await orders came down to headquarters. More definite instructions eventually arrived, along with the cheering news that the initial advance had gone well and fresh troops were required to exploit the successes. From the Brickfields the battalion marched to Usna Hill where it joined the 42nd Bn, who were likewise detailed to move up to Courcelette.

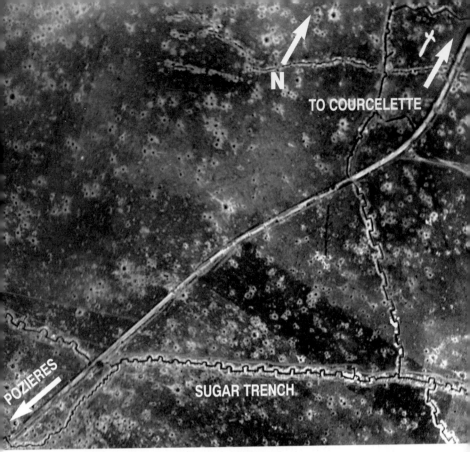

Sugar Trench from the air, September 1916. NAC

Lieutenant-Colonel Pelly, commanding PPCLI, was called to 7 Brigade advanced headquarters and given more detailed orders. An attack on Fabeck Graben would be made with the PPCLI on the right, and 42nd Bn on the left. Sugar Trench, captured earlier in the day, would be the jumping off position, but as the portion of this trench allotted to the PPCLI lay at an angle to Fabeck Graben, it meant that the battalion would have to swing half-left in mid-advance; a difficult manoeuvre at any time. MacDonnell Trench and the sunken road of the same name just beyond it would be the intermediate objective and from here the final assault on Fabeck Graben would be made.

Back at Usna Hill Lieutenant-Colonel Pelly and his men were just about to settle down for a hot meal when final orders arrived. Zero Hour would be 6pm which, like the 42nd Bn, gave the PPCLI only about four hours to move up to Sugar Trench. They therefore quit camp, and went up through the ruins of La Boisselle to the Chalk Pits south of Pozieres. A short break for the hot food they had missed at Usna Hill was made here before the last lap up to the front line. This took them to the partially sunken road running from Pozieres to Courcelette and it was from here that the attack began to take a turn for the worse:

> "The leading companies pushed northwards up the sunken road under very heavy fire. The Sugar Trench proved elusive. We never found it, and the leading companies came into action in strange ground, without realising fully where they were. We had pictured organisation in Sugar Trench, and 'jumping off' at the stated time. Instead the attacking companies extended to the left from the sunken road and moved forward to the first objective in open order." [15]

Lieut.-Colonel C J T Stewart. DSO

Major Stewart, leading the attack, looked round and found that Courcelette village on the right of the battalion served as a good landmark to place themselves on the battlefield. This was used to judge the direction of the advance, but almost at once they found they had overshot Sugar Trench and were already amongst the Germans, who popped up from concealed positions and shell-holes. But,

> "... the German troops which the Brigade encountered on this day were of very poor quality, and none of them except the machine-gunners had much heart left... had the enemy been officered and controlled the two companies might well have been wiped out before the line was straightened." [16]

The Germans threw up their hands and some seventy-five prisoners were taken. The advance continued; a communication trench was discovered and the first objective, MacDonnell Trench, was reached by 6.15 pm with only a handful of casualties.

The next objective – Fabeck Graben – was much more elusive. The

Captured Germans make their way to the rear, past a British tank in the background.

ground before the PPCLI was pock-marked with shell-holes and raked by small arms fire. The two leading companies advancing on Fabeck Graben now suffered heavy casualties, losing all but one of their officers within 200 yards of the safety of MacDonnell Trench and MacDonnell road. But a few platoons of Number 1 Company on the left had entered Fabeck Graben and met up with elements of the 42nd Bn who had successfully taken their part of the German trench line. From here the PPCLI bombed their way up 200 yards of the trench to where it joined Zollern Graben, while on the right some bays of Fabeck Graben were occupied close to Courcelette village. The remainder of the trench was still in German hands. Major Stewart, now one of the few officers left, organised the men to dig in on the positions they had already captured and await the arrival of the 49th Bn whom he knew were detailed to move up and attack Zollern Graben. To attempt any further advance himself with the men left would be futile. By the late evening PPCLI patrols on the right had met up with similar groups of men from the 25th Bn on the eastern outskirts of Courcelette village and a rough defence line was established. Major Stewart and his men settled down to what rest they could find until the fighting moved on the next day.

25th Bn

As the PPCLI were advancing on Fabeck Graben, to their immediate right the 25th Bn (Nova Scotia Rifles), commanded by Lieutenant-Colonel E. Hilliam, were moving in on Courcelette village itself. D and A Companies, commanded respectively by Majors Brooks and Tupper, led the attack. In extended order the battalion occupied

The western outskirts of Courcelette, assaulted by the 25th Bn on 15th September 1916. NAC

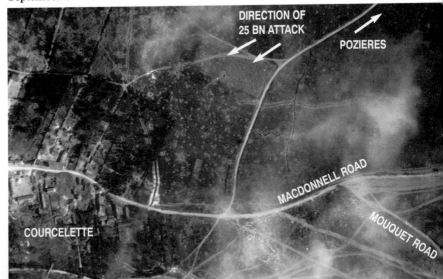

DIRECTION OF
25 BN ATTACK

POZIERES

MACDONNELL ROAD

MOUQUET ROAD

COURCELETTE

a frontage of almost half a mile, but they swept on, despite the German barrage which then raked the battlefield. The tangle of shell-holes around them added to their difficulties, but the Nova Scotians kept their formation as Courcelette came into view.

About 600 yards from the edge of the village German machine-guns opened up on the leading waves and Major Brooks was killed, along with Captain Dickey, the adjutant.[17] But still the men pressed on and 200 yards from the first house Lieutenant-Colonel Hilliam gave the order to charge and the eastern outskirts of Courcelette were captured at the point of the bayonet. The line was then extended to the sunken road on the left, Mouquet Road, and patrols eventually met up with the PPCLI in a portion of Fabeck Graben. The 25th Bn's attack had been so successful that they ran into their own barrage at one stage and,

> "... Colonel Hilliam, therefore, halted them, under cover of the cottages and garden walls, to take breath for the next thrust. He moved through the ranks, talking to each man personally, and found that in spite of their casualties, they had small need of cheering or encouragement. Amid toppling walls and hurtling death and a pandemonium that no words can describe, they were smoking and chaffing as if their halt was a mere route-march rest along a peaceful roadside. But under this gay and laughing surface was the thrill of a fierce exultation, and, in the words of their commander, they were 'like hounds straining on the leash' for the renewal of the attack." [18]

The Canadian barrage moved on, and the 25th Bn went forward again towards its final objective, in a valley some 300 yards north of Courcelette. Here they dug in and while doing so Lieutenant-Colonel Hilliam was wounded, although he stayed with his men. Parties of German soldiers were seen fleeing up the slope before them, and the battalion Lewis gunners and sharpshooters soon dealt with them. However, here the 25th Bn stayed, to await further orders.

Other Units Involved

Elsewhere the rest of Courcelette was being carried by men of the

The main street of Courcelette under German occupation. TOM GUDMESTAD

Canadian Corps. Elements of the 26th Bn pushing through the ruins encountered Germans who quickly threw down their weapons and cried 'Kamerad'. They were ordered to the rear un-escorted, as guards could not be spared. However, it was found that many of these prisoners were soon picking up rifles again and began sniping the Canadians from gardens and cellars, causing much confusion. One such sniper climbed the remains of the church spire and continued to pick off Canadians until late on the 16th September when he was dealt with by a party of bombers.

The 22nd Bn ('Van-Doos'), the famous French-Canadians, were also brought up and attacked the village with the usual spirit of 'elan' for which they were renowned. Despite heavy casualties, they captured over 300 prisoners and held onto a tight position between the sunken road east of Courcelette and the quarry. Among the prisoners taken were two German colonels and a titled officer, who retained his arrogance and superiority until Lieutenant-Colonel T.L. Tremblay DSO, the 22nd Bn's commanding officer, threw him in the prisoner cage along with the other ranks. It was later recalled many years later this German officer's

> *"... first contact with the Canadians gave him a small lesson in humility."*[19]

In the village itself it was found that,

> *"... this kind of fighting, this battling through the maze of half-ruined cottages, wrecked gardens, and tumbled walls was exactly to the taste of these eager and wiry Frenchmen. The variety of it, the scope it offered to individual adventure appealed to them. Into such individual adventure they threw themselves with zest. A fiery sergeant, having captured a store of German bombs, loaded himself with them and set out to put them to the best possible use. He bombed a dug-out crowded with Huns. He rushed on to another and cleaned it up with equal effectiveness. He then, still single-handed, attacked a third, but was shot down before he could throw his bomb. In spite of the heavy casualties which they suffered from beginning to end of their advance, the French-Canadians carried it through at a pitch of enthusiasm which made devotion easy and sacrifice of no account."* [20]

Courcelette village after it had been stormed by the French Canadian battalion.

Courcelette was now in Canadian hands – in an operation far more successful than Byng could have hoped for, and indeed arguably among the most successful along the whole front in the Battle of Flers-Courcelette. The prize was taken; now the Canadians must hold on to Courcelette and to do that they had to push out and capture Zollern Graben and beyond it – Regina Trench.

Chapter Notes

1. Corrigall, D.J, *The Twentieth: History of the 20th Canadian Infantry Battalion (Central Ontario Regiment) C.E.F. in the Great War 1914-1919* (Stone & Cox Ltd 1935) p.79.
2. Roberts, C.G.D. *Canada In Flanders: Volume III* (1918) p.39-40.
3. Loghrin, Major Samuel Monteith. 18th Bn. KiA 15th September 1916. Commemorated Vimy Memorial.
4. Robb, Pte John. 21st Bn. KiA 15th September 1916. Commemorated Vimy Memorial.
5. Miller, Captain Albert Peter. 21st Bn. MC awarded for St Eloi March 1916; Bar to MC awarded for Courcelette September 1916. Awarded DSO for Hill 70, August 1917. Survived the war.
6. It is possible that this was a stray soldier from the 15th (Scottish) Division, who were attacking on the right flank of the Canadians.
7. Lance Cattermole ROI became a distinguished artist in later life, and served as a commissioned officer in the Home Guard during the Second World War. He died in 1992.
8. Robb *The Journal of Private Fraser* p.205-208.
9. 'Report of Operations of the tanks of No 1 Section "C" Company H.S.M.G.C. 16th September 1916' in Canadian Corps Headquarters War Diary PRO WO95/1047.
10. ibid.
11. Topp, C.B. *The 42nd Battalion C.E.F. Royal Highlanders of Canada in the Great War* (Gazette Printing Co 1932) p.77.
12. ibid. p.79.
13. ibid.
14. Williams, R.H. *Princess Patricia's Canadian Light Infantry 1914-1919* (R.R.Clark Ltd 1923) p.151.
15. ibid. p.163-164.
16. ibid. p.164-165.
17. Brooks, Major Ernest John. 25th Bn. KiA 15th September 1916. Commemorated Vimy Memorial. Dickey, Captain Horace Arthur. 25th Bn. dow 15th September 1916. Buried Albert Communal Cemetery Extension.
18. Roberts op cit. p. 58.
19. Boissonnault, C. & Lamontagne, L. *Historie du 22e Regiment* (Editions de Pelican 1964) p.28.
20. Roberts op cit. p.56.

Some of the German prisoners captured at Courcelette, 15th September 1916. NAC

Chapter Three

CARRYING ON – ZOLLERN GRABEN AND THIEPVAL RIDGE 16 – 26 SEPTEMBER 1916

The Attack Resumed: 16th September 1916

On the morning of 16th September, Lieutenant-Colonel Cantile's 42nd Bn and Major Stewart's men of the PPCLI were occupying positions in and around Fabeck Graben west of Courcelette. Close by were Lieutenant-Colonel Griesebach's 49th Bn. Ahead of them across the high ground was the now strongly held Zollern Graben, a long trench which ran from Zollern Redoubt, north of Mouquet Farm, to where it joined Fabeck Graben on the outskirts of Courcelette village. An attack on this position was therefore organised by these units of 7th Brigade. It was to give a foretaste of operations to come at Courcelette and proved nowhere near as successful as the attack of 15th September. The poor quality troops encountered in Fabeck Graben the day before had gone, and the German positions strengthened. The 42nd Bn made their attack on the late afternoon of 16th September, and it was witnessed by one of the battalion chaplains, Rev. G.G.D. Kilpatrick,

> "In accordance with arrangements for the attack the first wave ... were to go over at 4.55 pm and advance as far as possible before the artillery barrage lifted. The 2nd line ... was to follow at fifty yards distance. The artillery preparation would seem to have been insufficient to break up the defence, and the enemy had, according to reports from air scouts, already massed large bodies of troops for counter-attack on our position. At any rate the evidence of those engaged in the attack makes it clear that the enemy's position was strongly supported by troops, ready and armed to meet this advance, for when the second wave of attack left their position the enemy could be plainly seen standing breast high behind the parapet. It was only then that the full realisation of the situation became clear to those in command. An objective which normally would have been within our power to attain swiftly and decisively had been transformed to a critical, if not impossible, task.
>
> There was, however, no alternative, for the success of the attacks on our right and left depended in large measure on the

The smashed battlefield around Fabeck Graben where the 42nd Bn fought on 16th September 1916. NAC

advance of the 42nd Battalion. No finer appreciation of the men and officers of this battalion could be offered than the fact that to a man they responded knowing precisely the hazard, if not the certainty of being checked. Every man went over the parapet with splendid spirit and courage. Within a hundred yards fifty percent of the effective force were casualties, and it speedily became clear to those in command that further progress would result in little short of the annihilation of the force. The men were accordingly instructed to take cover in the numerous shell holes, and as opportunity offered were moved back to Fabeck Graben." [1]

Casualties among the 42nd Bn had far outweighed those of the previous day. In the leading companies both Company Sergeant Majors

and ten sergeants were hit. Officers fell at the head of their men. All around were stories of gallantry and fine conduct under fire,

> "... Pte G. Dunn covered the retirement of his Company during the action of 16th September...He alone was left of his Lewis Gun crew, nevertheless he continued to advance through an intense fire until he was well ahead of his Company when he proceeded to direct a hot and continuous fire on the enemy's trench. When the remnants of the Company were safely back in the trench Private Dunn remained at his post for an hour, firing repeatedly to cover the withdrawal of the wounded." [2]

Recovering the wounded was always a difficult task on a battlefield raked by machine-guns and shell fire, and Lieutenant-Colonel Cantlie recalled,

> "... no body of men deserve higher praise for their work in these operations than the regimental stretcher-bearers. At all

Red Cross trucks on the battlefield near Courcelette, waiting to take the wounded to dressing stations behind the front lines. TAYLOR LIBRARY

times exposed to severe fire, and under observation of the enemy, they continued at their work with a self-forgetfulness and courage worthy of the highest admiration. The work of Medical-Sergeant Owston was especially noteworthy. For thirty hours he laboured in the forward area under heavy shell fire tending the wounded. From shell hole to shell hole he made his way with utter disregard of danger, directing and organising the work of the stretcher-bearers. During this period he was three times buried by shell fire. In his courage and devotion to duty Sergeant Owston was rivalled only by Stretcher-bearer A.A. Murray of D Company, who went through the enemy barrage fire again and again to the assistance of the wounded, toiling un-remittingly until he collapsed from physical exhaustion." [3]

Meanwhile the 49th Bn was brought up to establish an advance post before Zollern Graben when it was realised that entering and holding

Canadian Stretcher bearers. Lt-Col Cantile of 49th Bn remarked, "no body of men deserve higher praise". NAC

A Colt machine-gun as used by the 49th Bn at Courcelette. Many units had these weapons before the Lewis Gun arrived.

the trench was impossible. Supported by the battalion's Colt machine-guns located in the sunken Mouquet Road, parties of men pushed forward and eventually dug-in just short of Zollern Graben. Some probed the German line here and there, and it was during one of these attacks that Pte John Chipman Kerr, known as 'Chip' to his comrades, lead a bombing attack on Zollern Graben. He,

> "... was acting as bayonet man, and knowing that bombs were running short, he ran along the parados under very heavy fire until he was in close contact with the enemy, when he opened fire on them at point-blank range and inflicted heavy loss. The enemy, thinking they were surrounded, surrendered, sixty-two prisoners were taken, and two hundred and fifty yards of enemy trench captured.
>
> Before carrying out this very plucky act, one of Private Kerr's fingers had been blown off by a bomb. Later, with two other men, he escorted back the prisoners under fire, and then returned to report himself for duty before having his wound dressed." [4]

A natural born Canadian, Kerr had worked as a lumberjack in Nova Scotia before the war, and joined the 66th Bn with his brother in 1915. Together they had journeyed to the Western Front via England, where the 66th Bn was broken up and was sent as drafts to the 49th Bn, then in Flanders. For these actions at Courcelette Kerr was awarded the Victoria Cross. He went home on leave to Canada in February 1917, with his just-wed English wife, to a veritable hero's welcome. The City of Edmonton presented the Kerrs with $700 in gold, a fortune then. However, he was quoted as saying,

65

Pte J.C. Kerr VC.
TOM GUDMESTAD

How Kerr's VC action was viewed by a wartime artist.

"... we don't go in for heroics at the front. If a man is chosen for the job, he does it and that is all there is to it unless someone sees him doing his duty and rewards him for it. Nobody thinks of gaining distinction. If a man saves his hide, he thinks himself well off." [5]

After the war 'Chip' Kerr had mixed fortunes working in a variety of trades, and re-enlisted into the Royal Canadian Air Force in the Second World War. A mountain in Jasper Park, British Columbia, was named after him in 1951, and he died aged seventy-six in 1963. His Victoria Cross was donated by his widow to the Canadian War Museum in 1975.

On the right the PPCLI still had a section of Fabeck Graben near Courcelette village to clear, which still threatened the position there. Major Stewart organised his men, and a few from the 49th Bn dug in nearby, and advanced on the German positions.

" The whole affair was over in a minute. Attacked from three sides, the Prussians had no stomach for a fight. Sixty-two of them jumped on the parapet with white flags crying 'Kamerad!', whereupon Major Stewart, whose knowledge of foreign tongues

was not thorough, is said to have shouted back, 'Ici, ici, come ici!' Our men in great excitement jumped out of the trench and rounded up the prisoners. Our own officers, fearing machine-gun fire, ordered all back into the trenches, and immediately sent the prisoners to the rear." [6]

Fabeck Graben was now entirely in Canadian hands. Estimated casualties in the PPCLI were nine officers and 300 other ranks. Among the officers killed was Lieutenant A.G. Rosamund who,

"... left an important business in Canada at the outbreak of war to go to England and enlist in the Sportsman's Battalion (Royal Fusiliers). After receiving his commission in the Patricias he rapidly became one of their most valuable and best loved officers. A few days before his death in action, although one of the oldest officers serving in the Regiment, he unhesitatingly declined the offer of a staff appointment which would have taken him back to England." [7]

Rewards for good conduct were also given out. For his bravery at Courcelette Major C.J.T. Stewart, who had so gallantly led the PPCLI in the forward zone, was awarded the Distinguished Service Order [8].

The lines now settled down until the overall position at Courcelette could be organised for another offensive, and fresh troops brought into the forward trenches. Zollern Graben still eluded the Canadians, but it would not be long before the offensive was resumed.

The Battle of Thiepval Ridge 26th September 1916

The next major offensive began at Courcelette on 26th September 1916 as part of operations officially known as The Battle of Thiepval Ridge. Two British divisions (11th and 18th) and elements of 1st and 2nd Canadian divisions would attack the German lines from Thiepval village to Mouquet Farm to Courcelette itself, in the Canadian sector. Objectives here included Zollern Graben, Hessian Trench, Kenora Trench and beyond that the unknown quantity of Regina Trench. The 8th Bn formed the left flank, their commander later reporting,

"Punctually at 12.35 pm ... the barrage was turned on and the 8th Canadian Infantry Battalion moved out of the assembly trenches to the edge of the barrage. At 12.49 pm the barrage lifted over the Zollern Trench which was immediately occupied by our troops.

At 2pm an untimed message, from Major McLeod MC, who was in command of the left attacking company of the battalion, was received at Battalion Headquarters to the effect

that his flank was held up. I therefore ordered my reserve ... to
reinforce this flank. This party arrived at Zollern Trench,
which had been given as its objective, almost without opposition
and immediately mopped up the trench and sent back a party of
100 prisoners.

At 3.27 pm messages were received from Hessian Trench to
the effect that the attack on the left had altogether petered out
owing to very heavy enfilade Machine Gun fire from the Zollern
Redoubt on our left, but on the right 'C' and 'D' Coys. totalling
3 officers and 80 O.R. and 2 Lewis Guns had reached the
Hessian Trench, were in touch with the 5th Battalion on the right
and held the Hessian Trench as far as point 97; also that the
Regina Trench was not manned and was clear of obstacles. This
message was timed at 2.15pm. Brigade were at once
communicated with verbally and one platoon of the 10th
Battalion ... were sent to the assistance of the small garrison of
the Hessian Trench carrying bombs and ammunition." [9]

Here the battalion held on until next day when,

"... at 9am as the situation seemed somewhat obscure I moved
to the Zollern Trench to appreciate. I came to the regrettable
conclusion that the 11th Division had not yet occupied any point
in the Hessian Trench and that it was therefore imperative to hold

MAP 7: Canadian operations Thiepval Ridge 26th September 1916. NAC

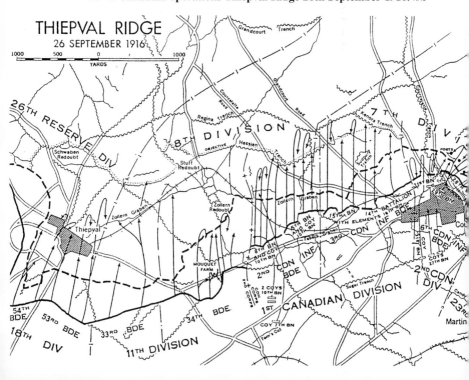

A smashed German position near Zollern Trench. NAC

our left boundary in that trench with a post; and threw back our defensive flank once more." [10]

The 5th Bn had meanwhile been advancing on the right of 8th Bn. The advance to their initial objective, Zollern Graben, would be shielded by an early example of a creeping barrage.

"The morning dawned clear and cool: there was very little artillery fire till about 11.30am when quite a lot of heavy stuff was fired into Regina Trench. The men had taken up their positions during the night in the kick-off trenches and numerous shell holes and were all prepared for the signal. About 11.40am the artillery opened up and ... kept up a heavy fire in the front of and on the enemy works. At 12.34 pm numerous Machine Guns placed behind our lines for creating a barrage behind Regina Trench opened up and sharp at 12.35 the artillery opened up with an intense barrage just in front of our men; this barrage gradually lifted and the attacking force scrambled out of their temporary shelters and advanced close behind it. Zollern Trench some three hundred yards in front ... was reached, taken, cleared and consolidated with very little trouble and quite a number of prisoners were secured and sent back, all of them helping to take our own wounded. The German barrage fire could not be said to have opened properly till nine minutes after the attack had been launched. During the advance quite a

lot of sniping took place and needless to say, no mercy was shown to the Huns who kept that up till cornered, and then threw up their hands." [11]

The next objective before the 5th Bn was Hessian Trench. After reforming in Zollern Graben the waves moved forward again, slowly following the creeping barrage for a short distance and then seeking cover as they waited for it to move on again. Casualties during this advance mounted, and only a handful of men eventually reached Hessian Trench. But the survivors occupied the position and made touch with the units either side:

"... it was decided that as we could command the valley and opposite ridge quite as well from the Hessian Trench that the Regina Trench could wait till the artillery finished cutting the wire entanglements." [12]

The call for the battalion to attack Regina Trench that day never came, and the remnants held on in Hessian Trench until the next morning when,

"... about 11am our artillery commenced to pound Regina Trench with the object of cutting the wire and it brought a heavy return fire from the enemy artillery. The left flank of the 2nd Brigade [8th Bn] had not advanced as far as the Hessian Trench on account of the 11th Division having failed to achieve their objective and as a result the ground between our lines was swept by quite a heavy enfilade fire from enemy Machine Guns, probably in Stuff Redoubt. At 11.45am the hostile artillery fire was very heavy and Germans were seen moving along Regina Trench and a counter-attack was prepared for. To help hold the gap between the left flank of the 8th Battalion, two platoons of the 7th Battalion were sent up from our supporting party in Zollern Trench ... The expected counter-attack did not come to anything and the enemy's artillery gradually slackened off to normal." [13]

Lieutenant-Colonel Bent's 15th Bn (48th Highlanders) had moved up to take part in the offensive two days before.

"... The Highlanders formed in Albert Square under the Virgin and swung up the road towards the white mound on the horizon that marked La Boisselle and the craters. The pipers played them to La Boisselle cemetery and then turned out and the Battalion went jauntily past to the skirl. It was as cheerful a march as any Somme march could be, despite the fact that all ranks knew they were 'going over'." [14]

Once in position Lieutenant-Colonel Bent met up with Captain Laycock, whom he had left behind in the line four days previously to form a burial party for those killed in the initial fighting around Courcelette. It had been a particularly harrowing duty, especially when the party had found a group of twelve Australian prisoners on the outskirts of Courcelette, lying in a row and obviously executed by the Germans. Laycock therefore,

Lt-Col C.E. Bent.
TOM GUDMESTAD

> *"... asked that his men be left out of the line. They had been living under front-line conditions for the whole period, without hot tea, on iron rations, and without rum – something always happened to it. And their job had not been an enviable one. The O.C. told them he was sorry, but men were short, and there was a big job ahead. He gave them a drink of Scotch to prove his regret. The R.S.M., not knowing about the Scotch, gave them a tot of rum, and then their C.S.M.'s, not knowing about either the Scotch or rum, gave them another tot, so that the party were the happiest in the Battalion on the way in."* [15]

In the attack of 26th September, the objectives before the 48th Highlanders were a section of Hessian Trench ahead to the left, and Kenora Trench ahead to the right. In front of them was Zollern Trench. Zero Hour soon came.

> *"'Fix Bayonets!' came quietly along the line and the numbing tautness of the last few instants can only be understood by those who know.*
>
> *12.34pm. The machine-guns opened with a storm of fire that utterly smothered a shout at arm's length – and it was on! It had*

The battlefield here was littered with dead of both sides. NAC

been unexpected, that machine-gun racketing, and for an awful instant seemed to be the Hun's. A long moment to wait and then they were going over the parapet in the glare of noon for miles, as the barrage opened with a crash that blotted the German front-line, the shrapnel breaking above it in rolling funnels of smoke and the H.E. sending it spouting in geysers of black earth. It was cracking down well beyond Fabeck Graben. The Highlanders were lining in No Man's Land under a terrific, unbelievable din that shut out thought. Faces were masks and men moved as they do when facing a hail of fire, like automatons, appearing unafraid but with a white, strained look of waiting for something.

They were well away. But something was wrong. Too many of those coming out at the junction of the old trench and our front-line were spinning and dropping though the Hun barrage had not yet locked down. And Highlanders fell just after leaping over the parapet, white knees showing and rifles held high. Then trouble was met in a breath, as it was always met in action. [Zollern Trench] was alive with Germans. Their bucket helmets were thick along the parapet of the trench which had been ignored as but a blind ditch. We had thought simply to jump it and go on ...

A bomber screamed to Major Girvan: 'There's a block – THERE!' pointing. Where the old trench turned there was a sandbag wall – German rifleman were taking swift toll from No 1 Company as they emerged from the front-line. One bomber's rifleman was killed. He was lying just under the lip of the block. Quickly, then, with the advance threatening to be held up before it started, Major Girvan and Bombers Frank Bradley and

Charles Duffy[16] ran a little to the right where part of No 1 Company were going on, unaware, and came in on the post from the side. They killed the two riflemen with bombs.

The three Highlanders were now looking down the trench which was well crowded with Huns untouched by the barrage, laid down beyond them. They were working their rifles frantically. They were fresh, in clean uniforms, and had undoubtedly come in during the night, likely under cover of the sudden artillery strafe. They were a sacrifice and were dying game."[17]

No 2 Company were being held up by a well-placed machine-gun, badly cutting up the leading waves. Major Acland, commanding,

Major J.P. Girvan.
TOM GUDMESTAD

Pen & Sword Books Limited
FREEPOST SF5
47 Church Street
BARNSLEY
South Yorkshire
S70 2BR

Would you like to receive information about other Pen & Sword Books?

Please fill in your name and address below:

Leo Cooper

Mr/Mrs/Ms ....

Address ....

.... Postcode ....

Please use block capitals

Trade enquiries please tick []   Telephone: 01226 734555

Please tick your areas of interest:

Pre World War One []	World War Two []	Regimental History []
Napoleonic []	Post World War Two []	Military Reference []
World War One []	Falklands []	Military Biography []

Leo Cooper

"... with the man or two next him, headed for the stub of an old communication trench. The Major fired up this with his Colt and a signaller near him heaved a bomb. It was a dud. A potato-masher dropped at the Major's feet. Another dud. Then along behind the trench came Major Girvan and the pair of black-headed, fighting bombers. They worked on down to the left, behind the trench, being joined by a dozen or so others, and had a wild few minutes picking off the Hun leaders. A hundred or so Huns were still fighting. But now it was over. A burly German officer or N.C.O. was ordering his men to retreat from the extreme left, where the trench ended. A few seconds more and the Highlanders in front swarmed over the stubborn trench and it was ours." [18]

From here the attack pushed on up the slope in the direction of Regina Trench, well across the crest before them and out of sight. It was at this point that the gallant Major Girvan fell, hit in the chest. Major Acland paused to shake his friend's hand and moved on, with the rest of his men.

"Just after breasting the slope, and away from the surprise of [Zollern Trench], *there had been a right-incline which was carried through in perfect parade-ground style, officers well in front of the line, blowing whistles which weren't heard. Major Acland gave the field-training right-incline motion with his arm and the entire left section of the line turned half-right as if on manoeuvres."* [19]

However, following this classic movement, rare in the heat of battle,

"... things were getting serious because of the casualties and the going became hard. The barrage was clamorous, though no doubt mostly ours, yet over every foot of ground men were twisting suddenly and queerly and going down with a crash of equipment as men do when hit hard. The machine-guns were mowing ... At one point a number of Huns started advancing towards the centre of the Battalion's line, firing as they came. They dared to within 20 feet or so, then threw up their arms or tried to run. Some of them got what they, perhaps, deserved ... It appeared they had meant to close with the Highlanders in the open but hadn't the heart to face the steel." [20]

The advance here was slowing up, and at a critical moment Major Acland was wounded[21]. The barbed wire defences of Regina Trench were tantalisingly visible ahead, but the Canadian artillery were only just beginning to pound them and the wire was still very formidable.

Canadian wounded from the Thiepval Ridge operations being treated in Courcelette. NAC

The Highlanders continued to follow a rolling barrage moving closer to Regina Trench, but instead of assaulting the position they established a line of advance posts opposite, forming a new front line.

> *"Shell-holes were being connected and the trench was deepening, with German prisoners sweating and digging as they had never done before, with bayonets jabbing at their rears to spur them on when they tired. The Battalion had changed in appearance beyond belief in that long advance of a mile or so of constant, isolated fights. But the task was finished and the day won, and all ranks were elated."* [22]

On the night of 26th/27th September patrols were pushed out to Kenora Trench, known to be out on the right somewhere. One carrying party coming up to where they thought the new Canadian front line to be entered it by mistake. It was found to be a deep and strong trench, and later that night bombing parties went out encountering isolated groups of Germans. For a while they believed they had entered Regina Trench, which Kenora eventually linked up with, but that position was to elude the Canadians for some time to come yet. The Highlanders hung on and improved the trenches of their new front line until relieved in the early hours of 28th September. During these 'constant, isolated fights' the battalion had lost two officers and 115 other ranks killed, ten officers and 213 other ranks wounded, one man gassed and another two taken prisoner.

Meanwhile in Courcelette itself disaster had struck the headquarters of the 13th Bn, who were in reserve during these operations. Located in an old German dugout, the command post was packed with the personnel that made up the battalion hierarchy; among them the commanding officer, second in command and the adjutant.

> "No one knows exactly what happened in that busy dugout at about 8.30pm. Who can ever describe a moment of high tragedy and disaster? All that is certain is that a shell burst in the roof and walls and ignited a supply of gasoline, the explosion and flames leaving death and ruin in their wake. All in a moment the Battalion suffered a grievous loss. Lieut-Col Buchanan was killed, as were Major Peterman and Capt Green. With them perished eight of the headquarters staff, while thirty-three others, staff and runners, were horribly burned or wounded." [23]

Stunned by the losses, and about to be relieved, the remaining officers of the battalion carried the body of their Colonel and the others back to Albert for a decent burial.

> " It was with heavy hearts that officers and men attended the funeral ... While all ranks shared in the sorrow and regret caused by the death of a beloved commanding officer, the sense of personal loss was accentuated in the case of those veterans, few in number by this time, who had sailed from Canada with the first Canadian Contingent almost exactly two years before. To them Col. Buchanan had been more than a good commanding officer. They had served under him in times of peril and trusted and looked up to him in a manner that bore testimony, more eloquent than words, to the very definite affection that existed between them.

> Canon Scott officiated at the funeral and the dead received all honours that grieving comrades could bestow. Military funerals are of necessity brief and this was no exception. When

Lt-Col Buchanan (third from left), 13th Bn.

*the beautiful lines of the burial service had been read, the rifles
spoke their farewell, the bugle sounded the 'Last Post', officers
and men saluted with deep respect and turning away, left the ...
gallant soldiers to their well earned rest."* [24]

On the right flank the operations near the quarry and the cemetery had
proved less successful. The experience of the 31st Bn here that day
serves as a good example. Lieutenant-Colonel Bell and his battalion
had moved up to Sausage Valley into bivouacs a few days before, and
he and his second in command had gone up to the line to reconnoitre
the ground over which they were to attack. It did not look good, with
plenty of opportunities for the Germans to lay down enfilade fire.
From Sausage Valley the 31st Bn moved up to the front line north-east
of Courcelette. Zero Hour came the next day, following a
bombardment of the German line, as elsewhere on the Canadian
front that day.

> *"Through this screen of dust and smoke the attacking waves
> moved forward, to emerge into a murderous fire from rifle and
> machine gun. Here was no dazed and demoralised enemy,
> crouching amid the ruins of his shattered defences, but a resolute*

MAP 8: The 31st Bn area of operations 26th September 1916.

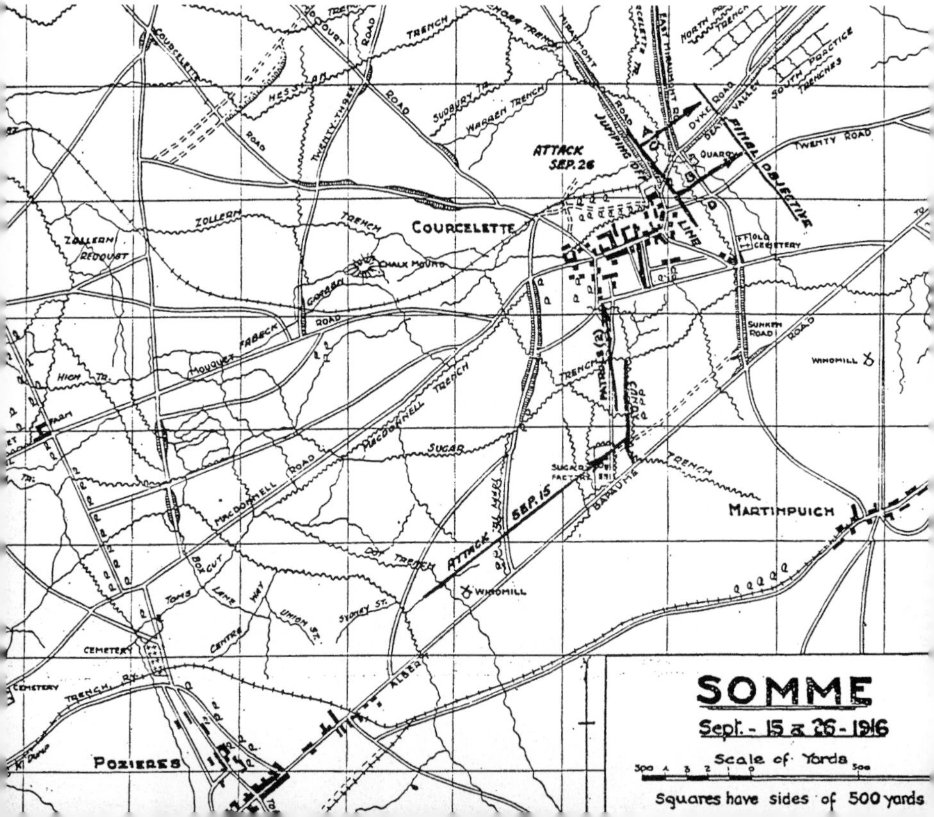

foe sheltered in almost undamaged trenches. The British barrage had failed in its purpose, and the morale of the enemy was unshaken. The defending forces were composed moreover, of German Marines, the best fighting material which was available." [25]

Some parties of the 31st Bn succeeded in getting close to the German line, but they were greeted with such a veritable storm of hand grenades and machine-gun fire that they could advance no further. Pinned down in No Man's Land the battalion could do nothing, which meant the flanks of the attacking units either side of the 31st Bn were dangerously exposed. Nothing, however, could be done and,

"... at 5.10 pm the Germans having definitely repulsed the attack of the 31st Battalion front, launched in their turn an assault upon the positions of the Alberta unit, which were at that time occupied by men of A Company. The German concentration had been observed, however, by the sentries of the garrison, and as the gray-clad troops swarmed over the parapet and across No Man's Land they were given a sample of the treatment meted out to B and D Companies. Such a storm of machine-gun and rifle fire met them from the Canadian positions, and from shell holes in which survivors of the attacking waves still lurked, that they were rapidly driven back to the protection of their own trenches." [26]

The fighting in the Battle of Thiepval Ridge had clearly been hard and costly. On the left flank the line had been moved forward to just short

Victorious Canadian soldiers returning from the fighting at Courcelette.NAC

of Regina Trench, but on the right very little had been gained. Ironically the Germans soon gave up these positions around the quarry and the cemetery and withdrew to Regina Trench. On the British sector the 18th (Eastern) Division had successfully entered Thiepval village, but the 11th (Northern) Division had met with many problems around Mouquet Farm. One veteran of the 15th Bn recalled his own and his comrades experience of 26th September 1916 well.

"It had been a rough 'do', though victorious ... Later horror, and some of the things they had seen ... were to come back to them. But they had to gird themselves now to the job of refreshing themselves and of working-in the rush of new men with all possible speed. There was no time on the Somme or anywhere else in the war to pause to brood. The old soldier appeared to forget most quickly for he long ago learned the wisdom of pretending to himself that he had forgotten." [27]

Regina Trench would provide many more opportunities and reasons to forget.

Chapter Notes

1. Topp, C.B. *The 42nd Battalion C.E.F. Royal Highlanders of Canada in the Great War* (Gazette Printing Co 1932) p.83.
2. ibid. p.86.
3. ibid. p.87.
4. *London Gazette*
5. From papers in the author's archives.
6. Williams, R.H. *Princess Patricia's Canadian Light Infantry 1914-1919* (R.R.Clark Ltd 1923) p.173-174.
7. ibid. P.177-178.
8. Stewart eventually rose to command the PPCLI and was promoted Lieutenant-Colonel. He was killed in action on 28th September 1918 and is buried in Ontario Cemetery.
9. 8th Battalion *War Diary* PRO WO95/3769.
10. ibid.
11. 5th Battalion *War Diary* PRO WO95/3767.
12. ibid.
13. ibid.
14. Beattie, K. *48th Highlanders of Canada 1891-1928* (Southam Press Ltd 1932) p.168.
15. ibid. p.169.
16. Girvan, Major J.P. wounded – survived the war. Bradley was later killed at Vimy in 1917, and Duffy the same year at Hill 70.
17. Beattie op cit. p.174-175.
18. ibid. p.176.
19. ibid. p.177.
20. ibid. p.178.
21. Acland survived his wounds, despite being hit again while being carried back to a Field Ambulance. He survived the war.
22. Beattie op cit. p.179.
23. Featherstonhaugh, R.C. *The 13th Battalion Royal Highlanders of Canada 1914-1919* (By the regiment 1925) p.134.
24. ibid. p.136-137.
25. Singer, H.S. & Peebles, A.A. *History of the 31st Canadian Infantry Battalion C.E.F.* (Pub. by the Battalion Assoc. c.1938) p.163.
26. ibid. p.165.
27. Beattie op cit. p.183.

Chapter Four

THE FIGHTING FOR REGINA TRENCH OCTOBER–NOVEMBER 1916

Before the Canadians lay one of the most formidable defensive positions on the Somme battlefield - Regina Trench. Nearly two miles long, Regina was the longest single named trench on the Western Front, spanning from ground south of Grandcourt as far as just north of Dyke Road near Le Sars. It was difficult for the allied artillery to range on, as it was sited just over a slope for most of its length. This also meant that any troops attacking it would be skylined, and therefore perfect targets, when they crossed the crest of the slope. Beyond it in the German lines was a deep ravine, Boom Ravine, an ancient quarry in which several battalions of infantry could shelter out of view from Courcelette. Branches of Boom Ravine ran towards Regina Trench, facilitating easy and un-observed movement to and from the front line. The trench itself was densely packed with Germans, many of them from hand-picked regiments. Thick belts of wire were spread out before it. The Germans fully realised the importance of Regina Trench and were determined not to let it fall into Canadian hands.

This, then, was the problem that faced the Canadian Corps through October, and most of November 1916. The first attack on Regina Trench began on 1st October, and there were many successive attempts until it finally fell on 11th November to men of the 4th (Canadian) Division. Many units fought at Regina Trench, but here the four main attacks will be looked at and key incidents from those dates examined.

The First Try- Regina Trench 1st October 1916

This initial assault involved troops of the 4th, 5th and 8th Brigades of the 2nd and 3rd (Canadian) Divisions. October 1st opened as a clear bright day and Zero Hour was set for 3.15pm. Two British Corps either side of the Canadians would attack other objectives near Thiepval and Le Sars. The main thrust of the operations at Courcelette was to occupy a line from near Destremont Farm on the right flank thence in a north-west direct to the junction of Regina Trench and the East Miraumont Road, and from here along Regina itself to where Hessian Trench faced it north of Mouquet Farm.

On this extreme left flank was the 4th Canadian Mounted Rifles (CMR) - a former mounted unit now fighting as a normal infantry battalion. Commanded by Colonel Gordon, scouts had been sent out

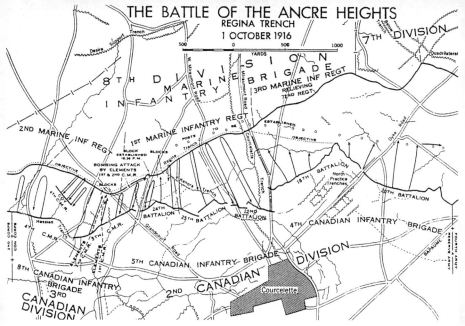

MAP 9: The Canadian operations at Regina Trench 1st October 1916. NAC

before the attack and reported back that the German wire at this section of Regina Trench was thick, and seemingly untouched by artillery fire. This information was passed down to 8th Brigade headquarters which ordered a further bombardment, but told Gordon that he was to attack at Zero whatever the state of the wire. Drizzle fell close to zero hour, but the men of 4th CMR,

> *"... itched for the word to go. The unbearable suspense made the minutes seem hours. The tension was not relieved until the ... barrage lifted and the attack was launched. A Company ... went forward into a blizzard of machine-gun bullets which checked them in their first stride. The barrage which was supposed to have been laid down a hundred yards in front of the enemy's trench had gone too far and the Germans, without hindrance, manned their parapets and wiped out practically the entire Company as it struggled to get through."* [1]

The survivors took shelter in shell holes as D Company came up on the right flank. Here they,

> *"... also met the heavy fire and never got through it. However, one officer and the remainder of the Company found ... the gap in the entanglements which lay on the left ... and fought their way into Regina Trench and held it until the last man of them was killed."* (2)

A and C Companies suffered similar punishment at the hands of the

80

E1D36

N

REGINA TRENCH

GRANDCOURT ROAD

TWENTY – THREE ROAD

COURCELETTE

An early aerial photograph of Regina Trench showing an attack in progress – on the original, sunlight can be seen reflecting off the helmets of men in the trenches and shell holes. ED STOREY

TRENCHES FULL OF SOLDIERS

well dug-in Germans, but by 5.00 pm the attack had developed into a bombing match from shell hole to shell hole. A block was established in an old communication trench leading into Regina, and here the 4th CMR bombers sent fusillade after fusillade of Mills bombs towards the Germans. It continued until their officer, Lieutenant Moore[3] was killed, and at one time a footing in Regina Trench was held until the Canadians were thrown out owing to heavy casualties. Colonel Gordon felt that,

> *"... the Germans had been more than prepared for such an attack. They were heavily reinforced during the action and would have been even better supported if the over-reaching barrage had not effectively found those who were coming up the sunken roads. The enemy signalled by red and green lights to his gunners who responded accurately to the detriment of the assault."* [4]

Casualties in the 4th CMR had been high - the roll call showed only 175 men left in the battalion. Meanwhile on the 5th Brigade front the 24th Bn (Victoria Rifles of Canada) launched an assault on Regina Trench via Kenora Trench. Operation Orders had been issued which dictated that D Company would advance on the left, alongside the 5th CMR of 8th Brigade, and attack Regina Trench from Twenty-Three Road. On the right A and C Companies were given orders to force an entry into the point where Regina and Kenora trenches met. At 3.15pm,

> *"... Major Parr stood erect on the parapet of the 24th Battalion trench, and, after waiting a moment or two, signalled with a forward sweep of both hands, that the hour of the attack had come. Immediately, in battle patrol formation, the waves of the Battalion's attack followed him as he moved into No Man's Land."* [5]

However, along the front of the 5th Brigade the result was the same. The advancing waves of the French-Canadian 22nd Bn (Van-Doos) were caught in the open by a tremendous German barrage, and concentrated rifle and machine-gun fire. A few survivors reached Regina Trench, but were all either killed, wounded or taken prisoner. The 25th Bn suffered a similar fate. Hit by 'shorts' from their own barrage prior to Zero Hour, the battalion still managed to assemble in No Man's Land and attacked Kenora Trench, forcing an entry and slowly moving up into Regina Trench itself. Only small groups entered the German line and were never seen again; the survivors attempted to dig in among the shell holes before the German wire, but swept by

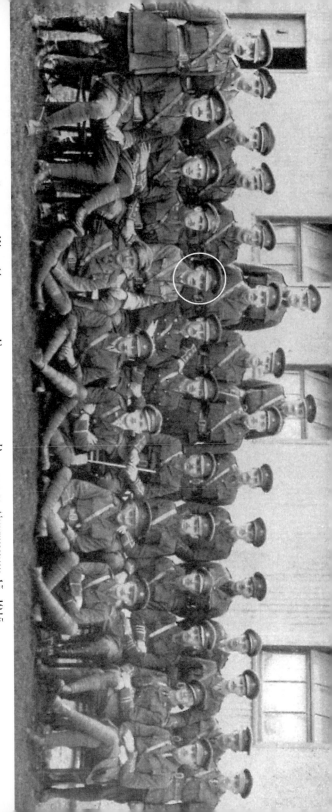

OFFICERS WHO CROSSED TO FRANCE WITH THE BATTALION, SEPTEMBER 15, 1915.

Front row, *left to right:* Lieut. P. L. Hall, Lieut. A. L. Walker, Lieut. C. S. B. White, Lieut. D. H. Beckett, Lieut. W. D. Chambers, *2nd row:* Lieut. H. D. Kingstone, Capt. R. K. Robertson, Capt. D. H. Sutherland, Major C. B. Parr, Major R. O. Alexander, Major C. H. Hill, Lieut.-Col. J. A. Gunn, Capt. C. F. Ritchie, Major E. O. McMurtry, Major J. A. Ross, Capt. P. T. Bown, Capt. B. H. T. MacKenzie. *3rd row:* Hon. Capt. H. D. Campbell, Lieut. D. G. Skinner, Capt. J. S. Jenkins, Lieut. H. A. Murray, Lieut. W. R. Hastings, Lieut. H. C. Kennedy, Hon. Capt. C. G. Armour, Lieut. Murdoch Laing, Lieut. I. R. MacNaughton, Lieut. A. L. S. Mills, Lieut. V. E. Duclos, Lieut. J. C. Heaton, Lieut. C. G. Greenshields, Lieut. A. G. Woolsey, Lieut. H. G. Davidson. *Top row:* Capt. G. F. Furlong, Lieut. G. R. Robertson.

Group photograph of 24th Bn officers September 1915. Major Parr is second row from front, fourth from left.

murderous machine-gun fire they, too, were forced to withdraw.

The 24th Battalion had also entered Kenora Trench, A Company fighting their way up into Regina until wiped out. C and D Companies likewise managed to find a small footing in the German lines but,

> *"... fighting of the bitterest type occurred in that section of Regina Trench between Kenora Trench and Twenty-Three Road, but beyond the road irresistible counter-attacks and deadly fierce shelling forced the 5th Canadian Mounted Rifles to withdraw. This exposed the flank of the 24th Battalion and contributed to the final enemy triumph in that area."* [6]

At the junction of Regina and Kenora some men of the Victoria Rifles of Canada established a position with a double bomb block, some fifty yards wide. German Marines were brought up to retake the junction, but again and again the Marines were cut down in waves by the dogged defenders. Here the remnants held on until relieved the next day. The unit's stretcher bearers cleared the trenches of the wounded, among them the gallant Major Parr who had so coolly stood on the parapet before the advance. Wounded by a shell fragment, he passed round cheery messages to his men as he was carried down, proclaiming 'did you ever see me with my spirits down?'. But several days later he died in a Casualty Clearing Station [7].

On the right flank the 20th Bn, who had been in the successful advance at Courcelette on 15th September, were in trenches just west of Destremont Farm. At the junction of two Corps, the British 8th Bn King's Own Yorkshire Light Infantry (KOYLI) were on their right. The staggered front line they occupied consisted of various sections of trenches, often not properly linked, and stretching some 1,000 yards from Destremont to Dyke Road in Death Valley near the North and South Practice Trenches. The 20th were part of the 4th Brigade attack, supported here by the 18th Bn. The objective was ground just south of this section of Regina Trench.

At 3.15pm the two battalions left their trenches, and in the 20th, all the platoons advanced across between 400-500 yards of open ground towards the continuation of Dyke Road. Once here they dug in and awaited further orders, or possible German counter-attack. Instead the Germans covered the ground between the old and new front line with a terrific bombardment, cutting all the newly laid telephone lines

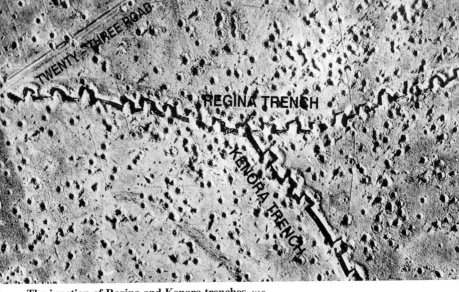

The junction of Regina and Kenora trenches. NAC

meaning the only method of communication was now by runner. Casualties had been heavy in crossing the open ground, but the battalion held on through the night.

Next day the weather took a turn for the worse and rain and mist descended on the battlefield. Captain Heron, who had already been recommended for his bravery on 15th September, took a patrol down Dyke Road to try and establish where Regina Trench was. At one stage he actually entered the trench, but as elsewhere on the Courcelette front found it too heavily defended for an attack at that time.

The fighting on October 1st had therefore met with mixed success. In many places Regina Trench had been entered, but not held and many of those who succeeded in this never returned alive to submit a report on the nature of the defences. The artillery had clearly failed sufficiently to damage the wire before this great German bastion, and it was obvious further attacks were needed. On the right flank the line had been moved forward by the 4th Brigade facilitating an attack on the trench here. Colonel Gordon of the 4th CMR felt the units involved had,

> "... upheld the established reputation of the Canadian Corps as shock-troops ... This was the first attempt to subdue Regina Trench. It proved to be no ordinary line of defence." [8]

The Second Assault on Regina Trench: 8th October 1916

A week later, a second attack was launched on Regina Trench, this time with nearly double the number of battalions. By now,

> "... the wire and the weather were more formidable

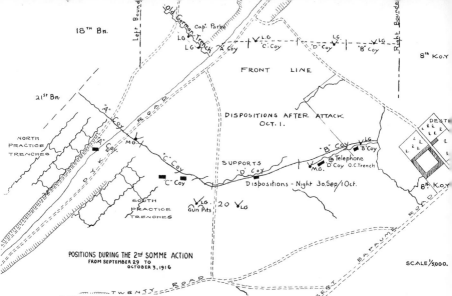

MAP 10: 20th Bn area of operations, 1st October 1916.

antagonists than the enemy. The ground, while not a sea of mud as it later became, was a foe in itself, and the entanglements, which were not sufficiently destroyed by artillery, remained as an inanimate adversary too strong for the success of any troops, no matter how indomitable." [9]

Into this were thrown men of both the 1st and 3rd Canadian Divisions. The attack was part of a larger scheme, involving British divisions either side of the Canadian Corps. The 1st Canadian Division on the right was to capture a line running north-west from Belöw Support Trench, west of Dyke Road, to a junction with Gallwitz Support Trench, then south-west to where the German lines crossed Farmer's Road - and thus the great Regina Trench itself. The 3rd Division would be directly assaulting Regina Trench from north of Hessian Trench on the left flank to the Pys Road north of Courcelette - here the lines of the two Canadian divisions met.

On the extreme left flank were Lieutenant-Colonel Griesbach's 49th Bn from Edmonton. They had fought in some of the earlier actions at Courcelette and now returned to take part in the operations at Regina Trench. At 4.50am a short eight minute bombardment of the German lines began, and at the same time cold, pelting rain covered the battlefield. Three companies of the 49th went forward with the RCR on their right at Kenora Trench, and soon disappeared into an "... inferno of shell and machine-gun fire." [10] An hour later Griesbach was greeted by an exhausted stretcher-bearer turned runner who told him that fighting was taking place around Twenty Three Road. He later learnt that many acts of great heroism were taking place. One involved Lance Corporal William Hannigan, from Peace River, one of the most adept baseball players in the 49th Bn. Griesbach wrote of him,

> "... he was wounded in the legs on the German wire. He crawled into a hole, bound up his own wounds and the wounds of two other men lying there; when German bombers endeavoured to bomb the shell hole in question he caught the German bombs in his hands and threw them away where they exploded without injury. Subsequently he crawled away from his shell hole and was again bombed; endeavouring to catch and throw these latter bombs away one of them exploded in his hands, tearing his stomach open and exposing his intestines. To keep his intestines in his body he had to crawl backwards in a sitting position and in this manner succeeded in reaching our trench." [11]

Hannigan made it to a Field Ambulance but his fate is not known [12].

Griesbach eventually made contact with some of his men and learned that none of them had succeeded in getting into Regina Trench. Of D Company, he knew nothing.

> "The peculiar, and up to the present unexplained incident, is the disappearance of practically the whole of my D Company and the left half of my C Company. They went straight for the objective; they disappeared over the crest of the ridge and have

MAP 11 : The second assault on Regina Trench, 8th October 1916. NAC

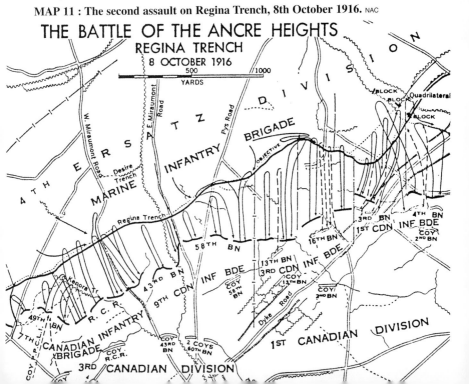

*not been seen since. Twelve men of D Company, under the
Company Sergeant Major, found themselves in Kendal Sap. Lieut
Balfour was seen to fall upon the enemy parapet. Lieut N.
Murray, commanding, was seen advancing alone apparently
dazed, towards the enemy trench. Not many dead or wounded of
this Company have been found, although the ground has been
covered up to the German wire, nor was the sound of protracted
bombing or small arms fighting heard from that direction."* [13]

Although the exact fate of this men in D Company is unclear, it seems
they were overwhelmed either by the German wire or in Regina Trench
itself. Lieutenant Murray was killed[14] and Lieutenant Balfour taken
prisoner along with thirteen other men of the battalion. The fate of the
others remains a mystery. The battalion diary for the 8th October
recorded sixty-one missing among thirty-nine killed and 103 wounded;
but the information Griesbach received that day was evidently
confused and the numbers may have been greater.

To the right of 49th Bn, the Royal Canadian Regiment (RCR) were
moving forward on Kenora Trench. A and C Companies pushed on and
entered Regina Trench, while D Company made for the junction of
Kenora-Regina. In this latter area the RCRs were less successful; uncut
wire and heavy machine-gun fire prevented D Company from reaching
its objective. Meanwhile in Regina Trench itself the two other
companies were bombing their way down the German position,
blowing dugouts as they went and taking a number of prisoners. The
section of trench taken in those early hours of 8th October was then
turned over for defence and posts established fifty yards beyond,
screening any German counter-attacks. These soon came but the RCRs
saw them off, inflicting heavy losses on the enemy.

However, it soon became apparent that both flanks were 'in the air'
and that the Canadian attacks either side of the RCR had failed. This
left them in a dangerous salient - counter-attacks were now coming on
from three sides and men were falling fast. A bombing party under
Captain Spate and Lieutenant Dickson was sent down to try and meet
up with the 49th Bn on the left. No sooner had they set off, than a
German stick grenade flew over Captain Spate's head and exploded in
front of Dickson, badly wounding him. A second bomb wounded him
again, and in great pain he crawled out of the trench, through the
German wire and out into a shell hole until he was picked up later that
night. Spate, himself wounded by the second bomb, continued to lead
the remainder of his men forward in a desperate attempt to reach the
49th Battalion - fighting could be heard towards Twenty Three Road

but Spate and his men were never seen again [15].

By 9am it was clear to the few survivors that to hold on was impossible and in small groups they began to drift back towards the Canadian front line. Of the officers who had led this attack, only one returned unwounded. Indeed the battalion had been reduced to 140 all ranks - and among the casualties some 207 men were missing. The battalion history concluded of their fate,

"... the names of many, it was clear, must be added to the long roll of those who would return no more from that area of suffering and death that was the Somme."[16]

A British 'Toffee Apple' 2-inch trench mortar as used in the operations at Regina Trench.

Next in line was the 43rd Bn (Cameron Highlanders of Winnipeg), in their first major action since arriving in France. Like other units that day they were held up by uncut wire in front of Regina Trench, but managed to establish a small position in the German lines. One company then bombed its way up the trench towards where the RCRs were, but were soon hit by a German counter-attack and only ten men returned from the fighting unwounded. Disaster also struck at battalion headquarters in a dugout on the West Miraumont Road. A shell came through the roof killing the Brigade Machine Gun Officer, Captain McKinnon, and severely wounded the 43rd Bn's commanding officer, Lieutenant-Colonel R.M. Thomson, in the leg. The war diary records,

"... while the Colonel was being conveyed from the First Aid Post by horse ambulance he was killed by a shell which exploded on the ambulance." [17]

The battlefield soon became a killing ground. NAC

Thomson was taken back to Albert for burial; McKinnon's body was lost in the collapsed dugout.[18]

The 58th Bn, also in their first major action on the Somme, had been allocated a portion of Regina Trench that ran from the East Miraumont Road to beyond the Pys Road. They assembled in a jumping-off trench just in front of the main Canadian line just prior to Zero Hour, with from left to right A, C and D Companies leading the attack, and B Company in support. Their commanding officer recalled the action, which they later discovered was against one of the most heavily defended sections of Regina Trench.

"In crossing No Man's Land the left Coy. D, and the left half of the centre Coy. C, suffered considerably from machine-gun fire and had many casualties. Wire was encountered by all three Coys. at from 10 to 20 yards in front of Regina Trench. On the right the entanglements were barbed concertina wire about 4 feet in height and 4 feet in depth, lightly staked to the ground. On the centre [was] the same type of wire well staked with iron screw pickets and coils of loose wire placed on top, approximately 4 feet in height and 5 feet in length. On the left the entanglements appeared to have been more strongly built than on the other portions of the front. The entanglements had not been damaged by our artillery fire to any appreciable extent. On arrival at the wire all Coys were subjected to very heavy M.G. and rifle fire and all Coys attempted to cut the wire and force a way through. In the right Coy ... Pte Simmonds discovered a sally port the front of which was blocked, and forced an entrance by which the right half and part of the left half of the Coy were able to file through and ... gained a footing in Regina Trench, and working along it to the right captured and held for about 30 minutes 100 yards of this trench up to a strong bombing post about on the right of the frontage to be attacked by the battalion.At about the same time men of the left of this Coy discovered a small sally port in the entanglement which they and a few of the men of the centre Coy ... filed through and gained a

Shells explode on the Canadian lines near the Miraumont road. NAC

footing in Regina Trench, capturing same up to communication
trench on the left and connecting with the balance of the Coy. on
the right. For about 20 minutes this Coy. was subjected to
bombing attacks from the communication trench ... and to M.G.
fire and bombing from what appeared to be a trench about 20
yards in front of Regina Trench. During this period the centre
Coy. and the left Coy. made successive attempts to force a way
through the wire entanglement in front of them but were mown
down by M.G. and rifle fire." [19]

The Germans soon realised that those of the 58th Bn who had made it into Regina Trench were in an isolated position - the units on either flank had failed to reach their objectives, dangerously exposing the men of the 58th. A well-organised German counter-attack soon followed, and after a fierce bombing match during which every available hand grenade in the battalion was used up, the survivors were pushed out of Regina Trench and slowly made their way back from shell hole to shell hole to the jumping-off trench. The 58th Bn had been effectively annihilated, losing some of its best officers and men. Their Colonel recalled some of the many acts of gallantry in his war diary.

"Major G.A. Reid, who was in command of the company on
the left, and who, although shot in the stomach when about 75
yards from the enemy trench, continued to cheer on his men,
subsequently dying in a shell hole. Lieut C.M. Howard MC who
gallantly fought to the last, leading his men and cheering them
on at all times ... He was last seen still fighting, although
surrounded by the enemy. A/CSM D. INESON who, when his
Coy. Commander was killed, continued to cheer the men of the
company, and when it was impossible to proceed further, assisted
wounded men into shell holes and went from shell hole to shell
hole dressing the wounds of the men who had taken refuge in
them, and subsequently succeeded in leading three other men to
a hole where they spent the day sniping at the enemy, and drove
off a small bombing attack on the gun pit." [20]

One of the most famous attacks in the operations of 8th October 1916 involved men of the 16th Bn (Canadian Scottish), when one of their men was awarded the Victoria Cross. Colonel Leckie's battalion had lost heavily in some of the pre-Courcelette tours of duty at Mouquet Farm, but had been made back up to strength and were detailed for the attack on Regina Trench. Occupying the line north of Dyke Road, they had one of the largest stretches of No Man's Land to cross before reaching the eastern portion of Regina Trench. Advancing with two companies in the first wave, and two in the second, as in all Scottish battalions it was tradition to be piped into action by one or more of the unit's pipers. One of the youngest in the Canadian Scottish was eighteen year old James Richardson, 'Jimmy' to his friends, who came before the commanding officer on the eve of the battle pleading to be allowed to accompany the 16th into action. Colonel Leckie eventually relented, and gave his permission for Richardson to join the battalion. Picking up his beloved pipes, he rushed to join his comrades.

At Zero Hour on 8th October the Canadian Scottish moved forward into No Man's Land and began to advance on Regina Trench. At first the attack went well. An officer on the right flank recalled,

> "... looking towards the left, by the light of the bursting shells, I could see the Battalion advancing in long snake-like lines well between the two barrages; the 1st Brigade attacking battalions on our right were coming forward steadily in the same fashion.[21]

CSM MacKie of Number 4 Company was in line close to Jimmy Richardson.

> "When our barrage started, Major Lynch, Captain Bell, Piper Richardson and myself went out of the trench. After waiting five minutes we bade goodbye to Captain Bell ... and Major Lynch gave the order to advance. The three of us walking [sic] in front of the leading line; Piper Richardson on the Major's left and I on his right. The going was easy as the ground was not cut up. About

Pipers of the 16th Bn (Canadian Scottish).

half-way over I commenced to wonder why the piper wasn't playing and crossed over by the side off him to ask the reason. He said he had been told not to play until ordered to do so by the Major. On coming in sight of the wire I ran on ahead and was astonished to see it was not cut. I tried to locate a way through but could find no opening. When the company came up the enemy started throwing bombs and opened rifle fire. Seeing a big shell hole on the left I ran over to Major Lynch to ask him to get in there until I could get the wire cutters to work on the wire, but as I got to him he fell - shot in the breast. I knelt to bandage him but saw he was breathing his last [22]. Piper Jimmy Richardson came over to me at this moment and asked if he could help, but I told him our company commander was gone. Things looked very bad and then it was that the piper asked if he could play his pipes - 'Wull I gie them wund (wind)?' was what he said. I told him to go ahead and as soon as he got them going I got what men I could together, we got through the wire and started cleaning up the trench." [23]

The situation in the centre and left flanks of the Canadian Scottish was critical. Here not a single man had managed to get through the uncut German wire and were engaged in bombing and sniping with the well dug-in Germans. Piper Richardson was meanwhile marching up and down the line of the battalion piping as he went, and according to one account did this for a full ten minutes. On the right, access to Regina

Trench was gained through gaps in the wire, and parties of Canadian Scottish bombed their way up, eventually allowing access for the others. Once in the trench a fierce fight followed - the Canadian Scottish were up against elite German Marines, who had already fought well in other battles around Courcelette.

As day break came the few remaining officers took stock of the situation, and although they had taken a trench as directed, which they could defend easily, they were down to only ninety-eight all ranks, two Lewis guns and a captured German machine-gun, and only a few grenades. Indeed when the supplies of grenades were almost exhausted, the Canadian Scottish began to use captured German stick grenades on their former owners. Lieutenant Hart, the most senior officer left, eventually decided that it was impossible to hold on. He later wrote,

> "... then we decided to fall back. We had by this time not more than seventy-five all told in the trench, few bombs and little small arms ammunition, and both flanks were in the air. It was apparently impossible for me to get messages back to Battalion Headquarters or for Headquarters to get messages to me. Therefore, I took the responsibility rightly or wrongly of ordering the Battalion to retire. Retirement was effected with light casualties, the men being passed back a few at a time to the jumping off trench." [24]

Jimmy Richardson was one of these survivors. Coming back across No Man's Land he suddenly realised he had left his pipes behind at Regina Trench. He turned and ran back for them and was never seen again. After the action Colonel Leckie strongly recommended the young piper for the Victoria Cross for his bravery that day, but his VC was not gazetted until October 1918. The citation reads,

> "For most conspicuous bravery and devotion to duty when, prior to attack, he obtained permission from his commanding officer to play his Company 'Over The Top'. As the company approached the objective, it was held up by very strong wire and came under intense fire, which caused heavy casualties and demoralised the formation for the moment. Realising the situation, Piper Richardson strode up and down outside the wire playing his pipes with the greatest coolness. The effect was instantaneous.

Piper Jimmy Richardson VC. Tom Gudmestad

Canadian Scottish on their way up to the front.

> *Inspired by his splendid example, the company rushed the wire with such fury and determination that the obstacle was overcome and the position captured. Later, after participating in bombing operations, he was detailed to take back a wounded comrade and prisoners. After proceeding about 200 yards Piper Richardson remembered that he had left his pipes behind. Although strongly urged not to do so, he insisted on returning to recover his pipes. He has never been seen since."* [25]

Born in Lanark, Scotland, in November 1897, he was educated in Glasgow and came to Canada just prior to the Great War. His family had moved to Chilliwack, British Columbia, where his father was chief of police. Working in Vancouver, Jimmy Richardson was an apprentice electrician and when the war broke out in 1914 he joined the 72nd Bn (Seaforth Highlanders of Canada), later being transferred to the Canadian Scottish. After the war the Courcelette battlefield was cleared by men from the Imperial War Graves Commission. Many bodies of Canadian soldiers were found during this period and among them was that of Jimmy Richardson. He was laid to rest in Adanac Cemetery.

Elsewhere on the extreme right flank of the attack, the 3rd (Toronto Regiment) and 4th (Central Ontario) Bns of 1st Brigade had achieved some of the only success on 8th October. They were actually assaulting German positions east of Regina Trench at a point known as The Quadrilateral in the so-called Le Sars Line. Here they encountered a far less formidable enemy than at Regina Trench, and although on the 4th Bn front some uncut wire was found, a line was cleared from north of Dyke Road to the Quadrilateral. Unlike at Regina Trench, this newly captured line was held despite several German counter-attacks. But casualties had been heavy - after the action the 3rd Bn only managed to muster one officer and eighty-five men out of fourteen officers and 481 men who had gone into action.

Once again Regina Trench had eluded the Canadian

Piper Richardson VC's grave at ADANAC Cemetery.

Canadian wounded being attended to at a dressing station.

Corps, and at heavy cost. This corner of the Somme was proving a killing ground, but would continue to do so until Regina could be wrestled from the Germans. Its well sited position just over the slope above Courcelette had once again shielded it from damage by artillery fire. Indeed, Lieutenant-Colonel Griesbach of the 49th Bn reported,

> *"... our heavy artillery failed to deal with the enemy positions. One of my officers who gained the Regina Trench and looked into it, reported that the trench was practically untouched: very deep, very strong and filled with men."* [26]

The Canadian Corps was badly mauled by the operations at Courcelette and Regina Trench. Since 15th September it had suffered nearly 20,000 casualties and all battalions in the first three Canadian divisions were well under strength - some mustering less than two hundred men. Byng suggested to Rawlinson and Haig that his men should therefore be withdrawn from the Somme, and gradually in the remaining weeks of October the Canadian Corps pulled out of Courcelette and headed north for the Souchez and Vimy Ridge sectors - then considered 'quiet' areas of the Western Front.

The Third Assault - 21st October 1916: A Chaplain's Account

It was then that the 4th Canadian Division arrived on the Somme. Not actually part of the Canadian Corps at that time (in fact part of the British II Corps), as the other CEF units began to move out and go north its battalions replaced them in the trenches at Courcelette. Meanwhile the British 18th (Eastern) Division took over the line before Regina Trench west of the East Miraumont Road, and this became the boundary between the two formations.

Previous to the Somme the division had served in the Ypres Salient, but none of its battalions had ever fought in a major action. Their first experience of Courcelette came on 21st October when a joint attack by the 18th (Eastern) Division and the 4th (Canadian) Division resumed the fighting for Regina Trench. Two battalions of the 11th Brigade were placed in the line; the 102nd Bn (North British Columbians) were detailed to attack on the left, with the 87th Bn (Grenadier Guards of Canada) on the right. Immediately on the left flank of the Canadians 10th Bn Essex Regiment were to accompany them into the attack.

Among the officers of the 87th Bn was Captain Henry Hutton Scott, known as 'Harry' to his family, who was part of a large Canadian family involved in the war. Another brother was in the ranks of the CEF, a third became a famous Canadian poet and their father was Chaplain to the 14th Bn (Royal Montreal Regiment). This was Canon Scott, who had been in France since 1915 and was involved in many of the earlier actions around Courcelette. Canon Scott had not seen his son Harry for some time, and in mid-October, as the Canadian Corps were in the process of pulling out and going north, he was pleased to find his son's battalion camped close by in Albert.

"It was during our last visit to Albert that the 4th Division arrived to take over the line from us. I had the great joy, therefore, of having my second son near me for six days. His battalion, the 87th, was camped on a piece of high ground to the right of 'Tara Hill' and from my window I could see the officers and men walking about in their lines. It was a great privilege to have his battalion so near me, for I had many friends among all ranks. The Sunday before I left I had a service for them and a celebration of Holy Communion." [27]

Canon Scott.

From here the 87th Bn made their way up to the trenches at Courcelette. On the morning of 21st October, following a heavy bombardment of both artillery and from machine-guns, A, B and C Companies attacked Regina Trench with their right flank on 10th Street Trench. This time the operation was more successful and by 12.15 pm Regina Trench was captured. The commanding officer noted in his war diary,

"... a strong screen [was] thrown out in front, the trench bombed and blocked for 50 yards on our right, and a strong point established near the Pys Road." [28]

Despite several counter-attacks the positions was held. Casualties amounted to 281 all ranks; among them was Captain Harry Scott, who had died while commanding C Company. His father was resting in billets in Roellencourt at the time and later recalled the episode in his memoirs.

"I was given a billet in the Cure's House. He was a dear old man and received me very kindly, and gave me a comfortable room overlooking his garden ... Roellencourt was a pleasant place on the St Pol road, and quite a number of our men were billeted there. I went to St Pol to lunch at the hotel and spent the day buying some souvenirs. On my return in the afternoon I made my way to the Cure's house, where I found my room neatly arranged for me. Suddenly I heard a knock at the door, and there stood the old man with a letter in his hand. I thought he looked somewhat strange. He handed me the letter, and then taking my hand, he said to me in French, 'My brother, have courage, it is very sad.' At once the truth flashed upon me and I said, 'My son is dead.' He shook my hand, and said again, 'Have courage, my bother.' I went downstairs later on and found his old mother sitting in her chair with the tears streaming down her cheeks. I shall never cease to be grateful to those kind, simple people for their sympathy at that time."[29]

Next day Canon Scott was given a car and driver, and was taken to a chalk pit near Albert where the survivors of the 87th Bn were resting. Here he was given an account of how his son had died.

"On the morning of October 21st, he was leading his company and another to the attack on Regina Trench. They had advanced, as the barrage lifted, and he was kneeling in a shell hole looking at his watch waiting for the moment to charge again, when a machine-gun opened fire and he was killed instantly. As he still kept kneeling looking at his watch, no one knew that anything had happened. The barrage lifted again behind the German trench; still he gave no sign. The Germans stood up and turned their machine-guns on our men. Then the officer next in command went over to see what had happened, and, finding my son dead, gave the order to advance. Suffering heavy casualties the men charged with determination and took the trench, completely routing the enemy. When the battalion was relieved the dead had to be left unburied, but several men volunteered to go and get my son's body. This I would not hear of, for the fighting was still severe, and I did not believe in living

men risking their lives to bring out the dead." [30]

But the idea of going back for his son's body played on Canon Scott's mind. He knew what the conditions were like at Courcelette, and that bodies left in the open would be eventually buried by shell fire and lost for ever. By now his unit was on the move for the Vimy sector, and it was several weeks before he was able to do anything about his desire to return for his son's body - or at least find his last resting place.

In mid-November Scott heard the 4th Division had finished its tour of duty on the Somme and was coming north to join the rest of the Canadian Corps. He realised this might be his last chance to search the battlefield of Courcelette for Harry's grave. Leaving his billet at Camblain l'Abbe on foot, Scott managed to complete the fifty mile journey to Albert with a variety of lifts in cars, ambulances, lorries, and finally a motor-bike and side-car which took him to 4th Division's

The 87th Bn's attack on Regina Trench, 21st October 1916.

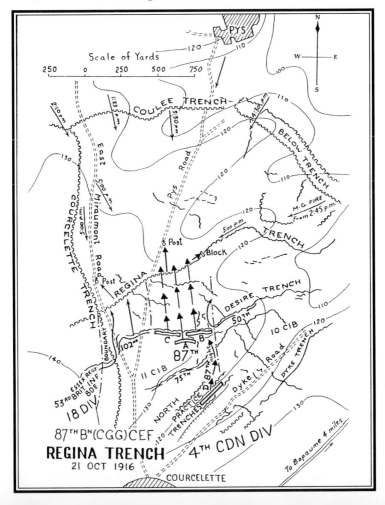

headquarters at Tara Hill.

> *"I told the officers there of the purpose of my visit, that I was going up to the front line the next morning, and asked if they would telephone to one of the batteries and tell the O.C. that I should arrive some time in the middle of the night. The Brigade Major of course tried to dissuade me, but I told him that I was going in any case, that he was not responsible for my actions, but that if he liked to make things easier for me he could. He quite understood the point, and telephoned to the 11th Battery.*
>
> *About half-past one, I started up the street which led to the Bapaume road. The moon was shining, and I could see every object distinctly. Near our old headquarters I got a lift in a lorry, which took me almost to Pozieres. There I got out and proceeded on my way alone. I entered a Y.M.C.A. hut and had a good strong cup of coffee, and started off afresh. That lonely region in the moonlight with the ruined village to one side and the fields stretching far away on either hand gave me an eerie feeling ... Not a living soul could I see in the long white road. I walked on till I came to what was known as Centre Way. It was a path, sometimes with bath-mats on it, which led across the fields down to the battery positions in the valley. Huge shell holes, half filled with water, pitted the fields in every direction, and on the slippery wood I had great difficulty to keep from sliding into those which were skirted by the path. Far off beyond Courcelette I saw the German flare-lights and the bursting of shells. It was a scene of vast desolation, weird beyond description."* [31]

Canon Scott eventually reached the 11th Battery's dugout at 3.30am, where he was given a blanket and a place to sleep for the remainder of the night. Early next morning he was up again, eager to continue his journey and reporting to the 11th Brigade Headquarters in Death Valley, a runner volunteered to accompany Scott up to Regina Trench.

The ruins of Courcelette. NAC

"He brought a spade, and we started down the trench to the front line. When I got into Regina Trench, I found that it was impossible to pass along it, as one sank down so deeply into the heavy mud. I had brought a little sketch with me of the trenches, which showed the shell hole where it was supposed that the body had been buried. The previous night a cross had been placed there by a corporal of the battalion before it left the front line. No one I spoke to, however, could tell me the exact map location of the place where it stood. I look over the trenches, and on all sides spread a waste of brown mud, made more desolate by the morning mist which clung over everything. I was determined, however, not to be baffled in my search." [32]

The two men walked backwards and forwards across the battlefield, in and out of trenches, occasionally peering over the side of a trench in case they could see a cross.

"Suddenly the runner who was looking over the top, pointed far away to a lonely white cross that stood at a point where the ground sloped down through the mist towards Regina Trench. At once we climbed out of the trench and made our way over the slippery ground and past the deep shell holes to where the white cross stood out in the solitude. We passed many bodies which were still unburied, and here and there were bits of accoutrement that had been lost in the advance. When we came up to the cross I read my son's name upon it, and knew that I had reached the object I had in view.

As the corporal who had placed the cross there had not been quite sure that it was actually on the place of burial, I got the runner to dig the ground in front of it. He did so, but we discovered nothing but a large piece of a shell. Then I got him to try in another place, and still we could find nothing. I tried once again, and after he had dug a little while we came upon something white. It was my son's left hand, with his signet ring upon it. They had removed his identification disc, revolver and pocket book, so the signet ring was the only thing which could have led to his identification. It was really quite miraculous that we should have made the discovery. The mist was lifting now ... we heard the crack of bullets, for the Germans were sniping us. I made the runner go down into a shell hole, while I read the burial service, and then took off the ring. I looked over the ground where the charge had been made. There lay Regina Trench, and far beyond it, standing out against the morning light, I saw the villages of Pys and Miraumont. It was a strange scene of desolation, for the November rains had made the battlefields a dreary, sodden waste." [33]

Scott and the runner made a mound where the body lay, and put the cross up on the right place. Now coming under heavy fire, they dodged their way back to Death Valley where the contented Chaplain bade his thanks to the headquarters staff and the runner, and returned to Albert. Some weeks later he received a letter informing him that some working parties of the 4th Division had found the grave and moved Harry Scott's body back to a small military cemetery at Tara Hill[34]. Canon Scott survived the war, though wounded in 1918, and visited Harry's grave at Albert on several occasions before the fighting was over.

While the 87th Bn was attacking on the right, the 102nd Bn was advancing on the left. They had come down to the Somme from several months of holding the line in the Ypres Salient and upon arrival at Albert,

"... every man exchanged his Ross rifle for a Lee Enfield and was issued with one of the new small box respirators which had come to take the place of the old P-H helmets, though the latter were carried for use in emergencies for another eighteen months or so. The new respirators were a great improvement." [35]

From Albert the battalion came past Tara Hill, following the usual route up via Pozieres to Courcelette. By late October constant shell-fire had reduced the battlefield to a wasteland, "... reeking with debris, human and otherwise" as their commanding officer, Lieutenant-Colonel Warden, later wrote. His battalion formed up in the line before Regina Trench, on the left flank of the Canadian attack with 10th Essex Regiment on their immediate left. B and C Companies formed the first wave of the attack, with D in support and A in reserve. Zero Hour was set for 12.06pm, and Lieutenant-Colonel Warden recorded,

"... at that hour the barrage opened and the men of the 102nd went 'Over The Top'; following the barrage like a wall, lying down until it again lifted and advancing as it moved, all in perfect uniformity.

The moment that the barrage lifted over Regina Trench the men were over the parapet; the assault was carried out with such dash, vigour and impetuosity that the Germans were completely demoralised and immediately threw up their hands in surrender. The first wave passed 150 yards beyond the trench, forming a screen; the second rounded up the prisoners and consolidated the positions secured, in

Captain Harry Scott's grave at Bapaume Post.

which they were assisted by men of the third wave, whilst the fourth wave was occupied in carrying up supplies from the old dumps to the new."[36]

Compared with the previous fighting at Regina Trench, the casualties had been very few up until the actual capture of the German position - only five killed and ten wounded. The Canadian artillery had clearly overcome the problems experienced in other attacks as the wire was found to be well cut and Regina Trench itself littered with German dead and wounded. Enemy counter-attacks soon followed, and it was here the 102nd Bn suffered the majority of casualties on 21st October. Each attack was repelled, but a heavy bombardment of the new line began on the morning of 22nd October and continued until the battalion was relieved the next day. By then six officers and forty six men had been killed, with eight officers and seventy men wounded. Few German prisoners were taken, especially after the death of Lieutenant A. Carss;

"... he went to succour a wounded Hun who treacherously hurled a bomb at him causing fatal injuries. In this connection it may be mentioned that all prisoners taken had bombs in their pockets, in their haversacks and slung round their necks." [37]

On the left 10th Essex Regiment had secured a portion of Regina Trench, and with the combined attacks of the 87th and 102nd Bns much of this troublesome defence work had been cleared. But still a section remained in German hands and troops coming up to occupy the newly captured position found themselves under almost continual bombardment from Miraumont and Pys. A few days later, on 25th October, the 44th Bn tried to take a further section of Regina Trench up to Farmer's Road, but enfilade machine-gun fire on the right flank stopped them with heavy casualties. It would require another full-frontal infantry assault finally to finish the fighting here.

The Capture of Regina Trench: 11th November 1916

A further attack was planned for midnight 10th/11th November to capture the final length of Regina Trench that still lay in German hands. By now the trench had been all but obliterated through shell fire, and both the defences and the defenders were in poor shape. The weather had got progressively worse and on the day of the attack it was frosty with a mist and low cloud. Three battalions were detailed for the operations: the 46th Bn (Saskatchewan), 47th Bn (British Columbia) and the veteran 102nd Bn. The objective before them was the block on the right flank, established in Regina Trench during the attack of 21st

October, to Farmer's Road.

The 46th and 47th Bns attacked at Zero Hour, midnight 10th/11th, in wave formation with two companies in each line. Some twenty minutes before they had moved right out into No Man's Land in preparation for the attack, unseen by the Germans in the darkness and protected by the preliminary bombardment. It gave them over 150 yards advantage when Zero finally came. The commanding officer of the 46th Bn later reported to Brigade Headquarters:

> *"At Zero Hour the heavy shrapnel opened on Regina Trench, and immediately the attacking party advanced ... At Zero plus eight minutes the barrage lifted, but the barrage was not concentrated over a sufficiently narrow area to enable the attacking party to enter the objective. The waves lay down until the next lift and then the attacking party entered Regina Trench.*
>
> *Parties of the enemy put up a strong resistance but were mopped up and many others who retired hurriedly towards Pys when the barrage moved forward were killed by rifle fire and by the barrage. Steps were at once taken to consolidate the new line."* [38]

On the right of 46th Bn, Lieutenant-Colonel Winsby's 47th were running into trouble. The Germans put up a stiff fight and casualties were heavy. At 3.30am the 46th Bn came up to their support and Regina Trench was cleared and consolidated. This proved difficult as,

> *"... the German trench now captured was found to be in bad shape and was so bad that it was hard to recognise. It appeared as if it had been held by parties out in front. Its dugouts were falling in but were occupied. It was well supplied with*

A smashed German artillery piece at Courcelette being inspected by Captain Talbot Papineau MC, PPCLI, then a staff officer. NAC

provisions, as though the garrison was rationed for some time. The work of consolidating and reversing was taken up immediately on entering, and every man worked with all his strength to prepare for emergencies. Good progress was made and a dry trench formed by digging down to the chalk." [39]

The expected counter-attack soon followed but was met with heavy machine-gun and rifle fire from the new positions occupied by the 46th and 47th Bns. A supporting barrage from the Canadian Field Artillery swept No Man's Land, but due to the close proximity of both sides there were many 'shorts', causing casualties among the 46th Bn. The Germans, however, were beaten back and the new line held. This section of Regina Trench had been successfully captured. Later on the 11th November the two attacking battalions were relieved by other units in the 4th Division.

The 102nd Bn attacked to the left of the 46th and 47th, near the block formed on 21st October. The battalion was still not up to strength after the previous operations against Regina Trench and marched into action with only 375 men; none of the companies numbered more than a hundred men. However, when the barrage lifted the leading companies were soon in Regina Trench and by 12.35pm it was reported at battalion headquarters that not only had the men captured their objective, but they had extended their front by 350 yards. Prisoners were already coming back, who were interrogated by Brigadier-General V.W. Odlum, commanding 11th Brigade, who had come up to see the results of the attack himself.

German counter-attacks threatened the position, but Brigadier-General Odlum called down a devastating barrage which stopped them retaking Regina Trench. Most of the casualties suffered by the 102nd occurred during these counter-attacks, but still the beleaguered battalion held on until relieved the next day. Together with the other two attacking battalions they had finally cleared Regina Trench; it had taken forty-two days and cost many thousands of casualties. Canon Scott, the chaplain who lost his own son at Regina Trench, had surveyed the ground during his final visit to the Somme front.

"I looked far over into the murky distance, where I saw long ridges of brown land,

Canadians evacuating a wounded comrade. ED STOREY

now wet with a drizzling rain, and thought how gloriously consecrated was that soil, and how worthy to be the last resting place of those who had died for their country." [40]

Chapter Notes

1. Bennett, S.G. Capt *The 4th Canadian Mounted Rifles 1914-1919* (Murray Printing Co Ltd 1926) p.39.
2. ibid.
3. Moore, Lieutenant Herbert Edward. 4th CMR. KiA 2nd October 1916. Commemorated Vimy Memorial.
4. Bennett op cit. p.40.
5. Featherstonhaugh, R.C. *The 24th Battalion C.E.F. Victoria Rifles of Canada 1914-1919* (Gazette Printing Co 1930) p.100.
6. ibid. p.101.
7. Parr, Major Clayton Bowers. 24th Bn. dow 3rd October 1916. Buried Contay British Cemetery.
8. Bennett op cit. p.40.
9. Roberts, C.G.D. *Canada In Flanders: Volume III* (1918)
10. 49th Bn *War Diary* PRO WO95/3867.
11. ibid.
12. The CWGC at Maidenhead could find no trace of a man with this name in their records.
13. 49th Bn *War Diary* op cit.
14. Murray, Lieutenant (A/Captain) Norman Grant. 49th Bn. KiA 8th October 1916. Buried Regina Trench Cemetery.
15. Captain Spate is not listed as being KiA; it is likely, therefore, he was taken prisoner.
16. Featherstonhaugh, R.C. *The Royal Canadian Regiment, Volume I: 1883-1933* (Centennial Print 1936) p.258.
17. 43rd Bn *War Diary* PRO WO95/3878.
18. Thomson, Lieutenant-Colonel Robert McDonnell. 43rd Bn. dow 8th October 1916. Buried Albert Communal Cemetery Extension. MacKinnon, Captain Ian. 43rd Bn att. CMGC. KiA 8th October 1916. Commemorated Vimy Memorial.
19. 58th Bn *War Diary* PRO WO95/3878.
20. ibid.; Reid is commemorated on the Vimy Memorial and Howard is buried in Adanac Cemetery.
21. Urquhart, H.M. *The History of the 16th Battalion (The Canadian Scottish) Canadian Expeditionary Force In The Great War 1914-1919* (McMillan Co of Canada 1932)
22. Lynch, Major George David. 16th Bn. KiA 8th October 1916. Commemorated Vimy Memorial.
23. Urquhart op cit.
24. ibid.
25. ibid.
26. 49th Bn *War Diary* op cit.
27. Scott, F.G. *The Great War As I Saw It* (Goodchild 1922) p.146-147.
28. 87th Bn *War Diary* PRO WO95/3904.
29. Scott op cit p.147-148.
30. ibid. p.148.
31. ibid. p.154-155.
32. ibid. p.156.
33. ibid. p.156-157.
34. Scott, Captain Henry Hutton. 87th Bn. KiA 21st October 1916. Buried Bapaume Post Military Cemetery, Albert.
35. Gould, L.McL. *From B.C. To Baisieux: Being a Narrative of the 102nd Canadian Infantry Battalion* (Cusack Presses 1919) p.28.
36. ibid. p.32.
37. ibid. p.33. ; Carss is buried in Albert Communal Cemetery Extension.
38. 46th Bn *War Diary* PRO WO95/3898.
39. ibid.
40. Scott op cit. p.148.

German prisoners taken by the Canadians on the Somme.

Chapter Five

THE END – DESIRE TRENCH
18TH NOVEMBER 1916

By mid-November 1916 it was evident that the Battle of the Somme was coming to a close, if only because of the weather. After the capture of Regina Trench on 11th November, further attacks north of the Ancre on 13th November had resulted in the capture of Beaucourt and Beaumont-Hamel, and heavy fighting was taking place around Munich Trench. At Courcelette the weather had got steadily worse and the temperature dropped to less than three degrees centigrade by 17th November, with heavy rainfall. Snow was forecast. One observer noted,

"... [the] *foe was the mud, the hated Somme mud, deep, slithering, tenacious as glue, foul with all the filth left behind by the enemy as he gave back yard by yard."* [1]

It was in these conditions that the 4th Division made their final attack on the Somme, indeed it proved to be the last operation before the battle closed for the winter. As part of II Corps, five battalions from the

The mud covered the battlefield by November 1916. Canadian 'Jocks' on fatigues along the Albert-Bapaume road. (NAC)

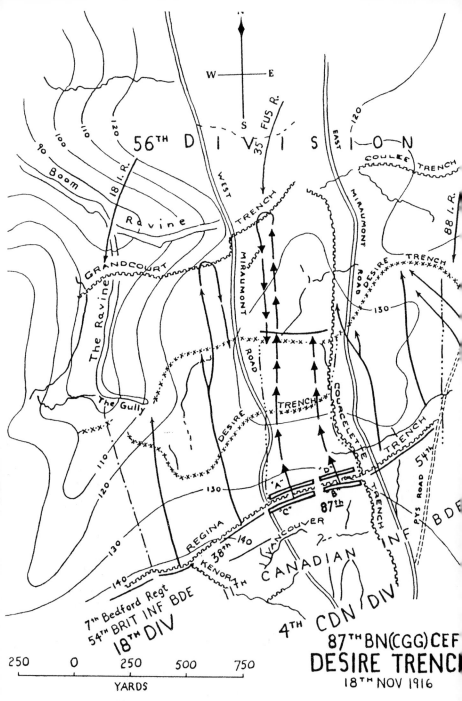

MAP 13: The last battle, 18th November 1916.

4th Division would advance on the right flank at Courcelette, with the British 18th (Eastern) Division in the centre and 19th Division on the left. Across the river Ancre, V Corps would go over with two divisions against Munich and Frankfurt trenches and other positions east of Beaumont-Hamel. The Canadians immediate objective would be Desire Trench and Desire Support Trench, 400 metres north of Regina Trench and at the opening to Boom Ravine, which in turn led to Grandcourt and Miraumont. From left to right the 38th (Eastern Ontario), 87th (Grenadier Guards), 54th (Kootenays), 75th (Mississauga Battalion) and 50th (Alberta) Bns were to make the attack on 18th November.

By now the heavy guns, the 9.2-inch howitzers of the Canadian Garrison Artillery, had been brought up closer to the battlefield and were dug-in around Pozieres and Courcelette, and at this stage in the battle were well supplied with shells. A network of light railways from Albert kept them fed night and day as they pounded the German lines at Desire Trench. The guns were clearly doing the job they had failed to do in earlier operations on the Somme;

> *"... the barrage work of the artillery was admirably co-ordinated, and effectually cleared the way...While a concentrated standing barrage was flaming and crashing along the whole line of the enemy trench, at the hour for launching the attack a creeping barrage was put up along a line 200 yards in front of our own parapets. This line of roaring death rolled onward at the rate of 50 yards per minute, with the first wave of our assault following close behind it."* [2]

These creeping barrages, common practice in later battles of the war, had been developed through the experiences on the Somme and although still being perfected, proved highly effective.

Zero Hour was set for 6.10am on the morning of 18th November. Just after midnight snow began to fall on the battlefield around Courcelette, and a whirling sleet swept across the lines which later became rain. Visibility was poor; practically nil in some places. Many of the objectives were soon covered with snow, which made identification of this shell blasted landscape even more difficult. An officer of the 44th Bn, in reserve for the attack, noted,

> *"... during the night snow blankets the muck and filth of the battlefield. From Regina Trench, men can look back across the valley they had set out to traverse in their ill-fated assault three weeks ago. The white coverlet that lies over the valley shows little hummocks - the bodies of their comrades."* [3]

On the left Lieutenant-Colonel C.M.Edward's 38th Bn went over directly opposite where Desire Trench met part of Boom Ravine, with the 18th (Eastern) Division on their immediate left and the West Miraumont Road as their right flank bordering the 87th Bn. Desire Trench was soon entered and from here Edward and his men pushed on into Grandcourt Trench, which they reached by about 8.50am. The 87th had fared equally well and also entered Grandcourt Trench and here they dug in and awaited news of the attacks on their right.

The 54th Battalion commanded by Lieutenant-Colonel A.G.H. Kemball, a former Indian army officer and British Columbian fruit farmer, was relatively fresh to the Somme, having taken no major part in any of the operations to date. On 18th November it advanced to the right of 87th Bn with the 75th Bn on its right. At Zero they,

> "... advanced under a barrage with a heavy snowstorm raging. The enemy was evidently expecting this attack and put up stiff resistance, but after hard fighting we succeeded in capturing Desire Trench." [4]

Lieutenant-Colonel Kemball was awarded the Distinguished Service Order for leading the battalion in action that day, during which it lost twelve officers and 201 men. Despite such a short tour the battalion's historian later recorded,

> "... On relief we march back to Albert ... This was our 'Good-bye' to the Somme for that year and it was with no feeling of regret that we marched out of Albert." [5]

On the extreme right flank was the 50th Bn, under Lieutenant-Colonel E.G.Mason. It advanced on Desire Trench, finding very little

Men of the 54th Bn at Camp Vernon, 1915. Lt-Col Kemball is middle row, sixth from left.

resistance in the front line, captured ten prisoners and then dug-in on the objective. Despite the weather all had gone smoothly until it moved on into Desire Support Trench where a further sixty prisoners were taken but the 50th then came under very heavy machine-gun fire which eventually forced it back to Desire Trench. Thirteen officers and 203 men had become casualties. Victor Wheeler, then a signaller in the 50th Bn, left a graphic account of this last Canadian advance on the Somme.

"Dawn's lustre was now almost completely hidden by a dense smoke barrage laid down like a great woollenblanket to conceal our movements. 'Over the top, men, and God have mercy on us all!' urged Signal Lieutenant Hextall. I clawed up on top with one puttee on and one puttee off. And we six signallers in extended formation with our bundles of 'A' and 'B' Companies, and volunteers from 'C' and 'D' Companies, scrambled over the parapet.

The creeping machine-gun barrage, magnificently and accurately laid down, paced us across No Man's Land as it slowly rolled forward, only a few dangerous feet ahead of us - like an invisible armour-clad guardian angel...The moment we exposed our weighted down bodies to the enemy he opened up with his light field pieces. As my small group of signallers waded through his iron rain of 77mm and 4.1 Hows across the open valley of No Man's Land, he also laid down his own terrific machine-gun barrageof 08/15s and 08s ('light' and 'heavy', respectively) that sounded like a thousand welder sat work on a battleship. His steel-core, armour-piercing bullets slashed past us like dense swarms of buzzing wasps.

My flesh seemed to take on an ethereal form, and the foe's death-dealing steel-tipped bullets seemed to be passing through my weightless body as we advanced across the forbidding terrain. A few silver shots clipped my tunic and ricocheted off my McAdam trench shovel. Millions of Boche copper-jacketed slugs were spitting into the ground around us.

Our objective was a wrecked British Mark I Swinton tank, immobilised on a distant knoll. It was aflame like a huge Olympic torch, lighting the tortured landscape for half a mile in all directions. For the past thirty-six hours billowing clouds of yellowish black-tinged, oily smoke, like fumes pouring from the stacks of a mammoth steel mill, had steadily risen hundreds of feet into the air.

As four of my men went forward on my left to take up their positions, one of them, Signaller Bill Farmer, was quickly mowed down by maschinengewher bullets, that were as thick as gnats on a summer's eve. Bill's work done so soon, the trio, daring not to

German dead at Courcelette. (NAC)

stop for the Dead, pushed on - and were soon lost to sight.

Signaller Jack Price and I pressed forward, but our chances of reaching the out-of-commission tank seemed nil. Yet, despite the machine-gun nests beyond, we remained cool and confident, determined to gain our objective in the face of almost certain death.

As Jack and I, who were on the extreme right of our Battalion, gradually separated ourselves from the main line of advancing Canucks, we came upon a partially hidden tank that had been battered to a Dante-esque standstill by a direct hit. A closer look at the iron monster, a lozenge-shaped land-dreadnought, revealed the annihilated crew, one officer and seven O.R.s, spilled out of the once-chugging steel fortress.

Only two members of the lifeless crew were whole, but they were deeply lacerated, as if by vicious pinking shears, and blackened by the still burning tank-oil that had smoked their clothes. One young lad, ashen as sun-bleached bones, was cruelly splashed with his own jelling blood. Other prostrate figures were grotesquely mutilated by the tank explosion. They lay stiffening in a zig-zag chain, one man's outstretched hand trying to grasp the next man's boot-less foot, and that corpse, in turn, reaching to clutch another's bandoleer.

Jack Price and I were already out of the protective range of our creeping machine-gun barrage which continued to effectively cover the main line of advance. As we pressed forward, continuing to veer to the right in order to reach our objective, enemy machine-guns peppered us unmercifully, and light field pieces screamed their curses upon us.

Rusty-tooth concertina wire ripped our clothes and tore at our hands. The recently deserted communication trenches made our progress extremely tough and dangerous. The slight but steady uphill lay of the land frequently blotted our view of the distant smouldering tank, and now even the five hundred foot high column of smoke momentarily disappeared.

Suddenly I realised that a dangerous gap had been opened up between our right flank and the left flank of the 46th, advancing simultaneously on our right...I watched the gap widening, nothing filling the breach except two very frightened signallers. On the horizon I spotted a group of the enemy - approximately fifty of them - advancing directly towards us from the now wide-open gap. Through my field glasses I could clearly see a much greater number of Allemands behind them, coming on very rapidly, extending themselves across the wideningstrip. If we had not already been seen by the enemy, I knew that momentarily we would be spotted." [6]

Wheeler was still no nearer the tank so decided, in desperation, to establish his signalling post where he was and with his Lucas lamp flashed back morse messages to the other signallers still in the Canadian front line. Just as the Germans were pouring down the trench towards Wheeler and his friend Jack Price, a message came flashing back across No Man's Land to get out. The two of them returned to

A Canadian machine-gun team take back their gun and a wounded comrade on a light railway trolley. (NAC)

their trenches and later that day Wheeler noted,

> " ...in the face of imminent decimation in worsening wintry weather, the slaughter mysteriously ceased, permitting the collection of human flotsam and jetsam. On 'B' Company's immediate sector of the line, both sides had mutually turned from fighters into reasonable men, and No Man's Land had become a temporary haven between two hostile lines. Friend and foe moved about with a divine measure of safety." [7]

Such truces were not uncommon when the slaughter was terrible; men who a moment before had gone all out to kill each other suddenly stopped firing and would go out into No Man's Land collecting the dead and wounded. During these truces the Germans often sought out Lewis machine-guns dropped in the course of the fighting; it was a weapon they prized highly in 1916, as they were often short of light machine-guns.

The final Canadian operation on the Somme front in 1916 had been moderately successful given the poor weather conditions. Desire Trench had been taken and held, as had Desire Support and Grandcourt Trench in places, but counter-attacks and machine-gun fire had forced these men back. On the right flank, as Victor Wheeler had testified, things had not not gone so well. British divisions around the Ancre had also suffered badly, but the 18th (Eastern) Division on the left flank of the Canadians had taken its objectives despite being worn down by the Somme fighting (it had been in the area since 1st July) and all its battalions were well under strength. In any case it was virtually impossible to conduct operations in such conditions, and after the attack of 18th November the British high command called an end to the Somme offensive. British casualties numbered 450,000 of whom over 24,000 were Canadian. Courcelette had become the killing ground of the Canadian Corps who had left over 8,000 dead on the battlefield. They were never to suffer such casualties again, and Major C.G.D. Roberts concluded in 1918 that the experiences at Courcelette, Regina and Desire Trenches had changed the Canadian Corps.

> "Welded now by sacrifice, endurance, prudent and brilliant leadership, and glorious achievements...into a fighting force of incomparable effectiveness, it was no less than their due that the most tremendous tasks should be set to these fiery and indomitable fighters of the North. To the Canadian Battalions the impregnable and the invincible had come to mean a challenge which they welcomed joyously. They knew that the utmost of which men were capable was confidently expected of them." [8]

An officer of the 44th Bn left a different picture, which could be the epitaph of any Canadian battalion on the Somme.

"Men are worn out. Many of their comrades are left in muddy graves on the battlefield; hundreds have been wounded; numbers have been evacuated sick and exhausted. Of the survivors many are minus great-coats, puttees, 'tin-hats' - equipment and clothing are still caked with the Somme mud, despite all efforts at cleaning up.

The battalion that marches away is very different from the one which swung so gaily through the highways and by ways of Bramshott. Seven weeks in the Somme battle had subjected the men to a terrible experience. All that the Great War could produce in hardship, suffering, misfortune, disappointment, has been mixed by destiny into one bitter draught." [9]

Chapter Notes

1. Roberts, C.G.D. *Canada In Flanders: Volume III* (1918) p.113.
2. ibid. p.116.
3. Russenholt, E.S. *Six Thousand Canadian Men: The History of the 44th Battalion Canadian Infantry 1914-1919* (De Montfort Press 1932) p.58.
4. Beswick, B.J. *Cinquante-Quatre: A History of the 54th Battalion Canadian Infantry Battalion* (1919) p.12.
5. ibid. p.12.
6. Wheeler, V.W. *No Man's Land* (Calgary 1980) p.52-55.
7. ibid. p.58.
8. Roberts op cit. p.121.
9. Russenholt op cit. p.60-61.

Chapter Six

RETURN TO COURCELETTE

Will Bird was a veteran of the 42nd Bn (Black Watch of Canada) who had been awarded a Military Medal for the last battle of the Great War, at Mons in November 1918. After the war he wrote many articles about his experiences and eventually recorded them in his memoirs *Ghosts Have Warm Hands*, a classic account of the Great War which has recently (1997) been reprinted[1]. Later he toured the old Western Front battlefields which resulted in a book *Thirteen Years After*. Part of his pilgrimage included a visit to the Courcelette area, and a journey across the old battlefields to Albert, mimicing a route followed to and from the line by Canadian soldiers in 1916. It is reproduced here, giving a vivid and unique insight into the Somme as it was in the early 1930s.

"Courcelette! It seemed but a small village as we stood and gazed over its roofs from the higher ground at the old sugar refinery. The refinery ruin projects in full view of the road, but mostly it has been covered by the building of a most modern establishment, owned by the present mayor of Courcelette. The ruin shows itself between the great barn and water tower. We went to the Canadian Memorial, which is on the right just before the village - beautiful ground with a brown hedge surrounding it. The memorial itself is but another of those stones such as centre the grounds at Hill 62 and at Passchendaele, most disappointing to the usual conception of a memorial.

We went down the slope into the village. The church is very new, and the memorial of the French is near by. The houses also look quite new, and here and there you see old cellars and low

The sugar factory in 1919. CLIVE HARRIS

The sugar factory at the time Will Bird visited Courcelette. CLIVE HARRIS

ruins. *There are three very large barns in the village, and the Mairie is almost hidden by them. I went into a blue painted cafe bearing a huge sign, 'Tabac-Cabine Telephonique.'*

Madame greeted us warmly and was quite eager to talk. She is an 'original' of Courcelette, and told us of her life there during eighteen months of German occupation, and of seeing a German officer kick his men on parade. The British shells came very near and the Germans were remarkably adept at taking cover. After the people came back to the ruins of Courcelette and started rebuilding they found many German dead in the cellars where they had been crushed by the barrage preceding its capture.

We went outside and found a road leading toward Regina Trench. Going along it a distance into the old sunken road, we soon came to men shovelling earth on a winter cache of vegetables. On their digging they were very near the road bank and they had uncovered two German helmets, German long boots, mess tins, equipment and a few bones. They did not mind, they said, as long as there were no shells or bombs. Never did they plough or harrow, they told us, but they uncovered some debris of war. We found a section of rough ground, seemingly an old trench, and, judging from my map, a part of old Kenora Trench. There was not a trace of Regina, or Hessian or Fabeck Graben or Zollern.

We wandered away over toward Thiepval in our search for a trace of Desire Trench, and found none, or any war signs near

The main street of Courcelette 1919.

A grass covered wasteland between Pozieres and Courcelette, 1919. The view is from The Windmill towards Thiepval, and shows the old shell-holes about the O.G. Lines.

Mouquet Farm. On the soft ground it was a long, tiresome tramp, and there was not a trace of old trenches as a reward. Only those with very vivid memories could now point out the exact lines that were assaulted during those terrible autumn days of '16.

The Germans still talk of the 'blood bath of the Somme', and all veterans agree that for terrific shell fire among conditions of mud and water in terrible weather, the battle of the Somme was only exceeded in dreadfulness by the battle of Passchendaele. For every Victoria Cross awarded there, a hundred were equally well won.

Courcelette cemetery gleams white in the distance as you leave the Sugar Factory, and the blurred whiteness of two others are seen beyond. All through the Somme one passes countless cemeteries, British, French and German, until it seems a great valley of the dead.

Long open fields, and then we halted beside the Tank Memorial, four miniature tanks at the foot of a shaft. It is beside Pozières, a straggling village with many wooden huts, small houses, and a few big farm homes. Villa Victoria is the name of the only expansive front we saw. Just outside the village, on the site of the old windmill of Pozières, is a memorial of the Australians, and there is a monument erected in memory of some of the King's Royal Rifle. Contalmaison looms on the left, and Thiepval seems near on the right. Pozières British Cemetery is beside the road, and is a beautiful square of double columns, a splendid structure.

Now over on the right is Ovillers, in '18 but a mass of brick dust and chalk, powdered wreckage with nothing definite in its midst. It appears now as a pretty village, blending with the greens of its slopes, with long white rows of fence posts extending from the rear like white streamers; and the cemetery farther on is a shining square of whiteness.

'War ground' is plentiful. You see old gun positions and parts of trenches, and rough contours are frequent as you look over Mash and Blighty Valleys. Left and right, these old craters and trench holes become more plentiful, and then you are at La Boisselle in the very heart of the war-torn area. It is a tiny village. A few heroic ones have tried to reclaim that wilderness, but only the main street and another lane or so have resulted. All else are craters, shell holes, gullies, rifts in the earth, barren in spots of anything that grows.

To the right a gate bears a large sign, Fermez La Porte S.V.P. Going through it and over slippery chalk soil, you reach the lips of an enormous crater [Y Sap crater - now filled in]. While we stood there, a cart-load of tourists came. They were gazing all about them, remarking on the condition of the village ground, but when they reached the crater they stood silent, and went away saying very little. They had got a glimpse of war.

We crossed to the other road, went over it and out to the other huge crater [Lochnagar Crater]. All about it desolation extends like a terrible wound. In smaller craters we saw much refuse of war, and then in a shell hole probed at a leather end and found it to be an entire equipment. Near by was a water bottle and a

The Y-Sap crater about the time Will Bird visited it.

Wooden houses in Courcelette, 1919.

bayonet scabbard. A steel helmet, jagged by a shrapnel cut, showed where a rotting ground sheet held long German boots. Wandering around, we saw countless other relics, as if the place had never been visited. Below the village there is a memorial to the Tyneside Irish and Tyneside Scottish. They were in that vicinity when those craters were blown July 1, '16, and the great battle of the Somme commenced.

Going on, Sausage Valley looks peaceful enough, with three horses feeding in its pasturage. On the right is Usna Hill, and on the left Tara Hill, so well known to the Canadians. An open, featureless field extends where the horse lines used to be, and there were grain stacks on the site of the old 'Y'. The hills are a rich, dark green, and all that outskirt of Albert is most verdant looking.

Bapaume Post Cemetery is passed, and then we are entering Albert, mecca once for many weary battalions. There are huts even in the town, and long tenements. We cross the railway and soon are among new buildings of blue and grey and yellow borders, new concrete and flaring signs. It is all very modern, and the garage man who supplied us with 'essence' [petrol] tells us that Albert sees a multitude of tourists. Here and there we spot old ruins, but the Grand Place and its Hotel de Ville are most imposing. The cathedral and its new Virgin are very grand, and the station and its surroundings are modern in every detail. Albert appeared to me a very lively energetic town, eager for business. At the left, near the station, where the river shows itself, there is much war wreckage. Just outside in that direction all seems as it was, but on the whole the tourist must be impressed.

We had lunch at the cafe, A Tout Va Bien, and were served an excellent meal. At the next table was an ex-sergeant of Army Transport, and he entertained us with stories of war days. Our friend told us that over near Trones Wood a German was found

121

digging industriously about a year after the war. He claimed that a pay officer of his regiment had been buried alive there by a big shell, and that the man had five watches in his pocket, as well as the battalion pay in a leather satchel. He was rather rudely advised to stop digging."

From Albert, Will Bird and his companion returned to the battlefield around Courcelette, and continued with his observations on the state of the ground as it was at that time.

"Every village on the Somme seems the same, as if all had been rebuilt by the same contractor. Every one of them in winter is an eyesore to travellers or anyone outside the area. You disturb a huge flock of crows as you approach the place, pass a huddle of grain stacks, and are in view of a collection of huts. These look as if they had been hastily erected in the only cleared spaces that existed at the time, and there they remain.

Some of the wooden ones are painted, always a bilious blue or sickly yellow. Inside the hut suburb you meet long barns, usually cornering the street, immense brick walls with enormous doors in the centre, or else wooden walls, and, often, corrugated iron roofs. These barns are established with the same haphazard method of location, and the street or road seems to curve in and out to please them. Here and there the big doors are open and you view a spongy midden crowded with pigs and fowl, and get a glimpse of a bony female clumping around the brick or cobbled ledge of the yard. She will be carrying a bush broom or spade or pitchfork, feet in clumsy sabots and a scarf around her neck. In the corner of the yard there will be an accumulation of tools and poles and various buckets and tubs, and a yapping dog will be straining at his chain as you go by.

Go around the corner and there may be a brick house with a low wall in front surmounted by an iron fence, always painted green. Perhaps there will be three or four homes of a semi-bungalow type, with a concrete finish that has been painted various colours, brown and yellow, and a blue-grey. These have many ornaments at the corners, and all sorts of artistry about the windows. Beyond them is an estaminet or two, generally placed, with canny judgement, near the brick or concrete-walled water hole. There the thirsty drivers bring their horses at noon and have their beer. One or two shops, in houses, and possibly a bakery or barber shop, and you reach the church, brick or concrete and fantastic in construction or hideously plain, then the combined Mairie-Ecole, the War Memorial, and you are through the town.

The people, however, are voluble. They will tell you endless stories about those killed or maimed through disturbing explosives, about the things they have seen in old dugouts and cellars when first they returned to their lands, and they will talk to you of bodies found until your fresh crawls. Whether or not they have concocted such entertainment for tourists, I cannot say.

We went on out the sunken road and to Courcelette again. I wanted to have another look at the sunken road there. It is banked as high as your shoulder, and on top you can see the long white lines that indicate old trenches. A farmer came along, riding an immense horse, and asked what I was looking for. He began to talk as soon as I explained, and told me that he had seen at least a hundred bodies taken from the sunken road. When they had cleaned it and made it wide enough for traffic they found British and German weapons of all kinds, bombs, shells, everything, even to a huge cheese, under the mounds of shell-piled earth. Only last summer a boy had his arm blown off by a bomb explosion as he played in the Somme fields, and the farmer said he had seen an auto [car] blown from the road as it detonated a shell. It will be years before they can move with security in the old battlefields." [2]

Present day visitors to the Western Front might well compare Will Bird's description of a typical Somme village with what they themselves see today – how little has changed!

Chapter Notes

(1) Bird, Will R. *Ghosts Have Warm Hands* (CEF Books 1997). For copies contact: CEF Books, PO Box 29123, Nepean, Ontario, K2J 4A9, Canada.
(2) Bird, Will R. *Thirteen Years After* (Maclean Publishing Company, Canada, (1932) p.123 ff.

The sunken road at Courcelette 'Thirteen Years After'. CLIVE HARRIS

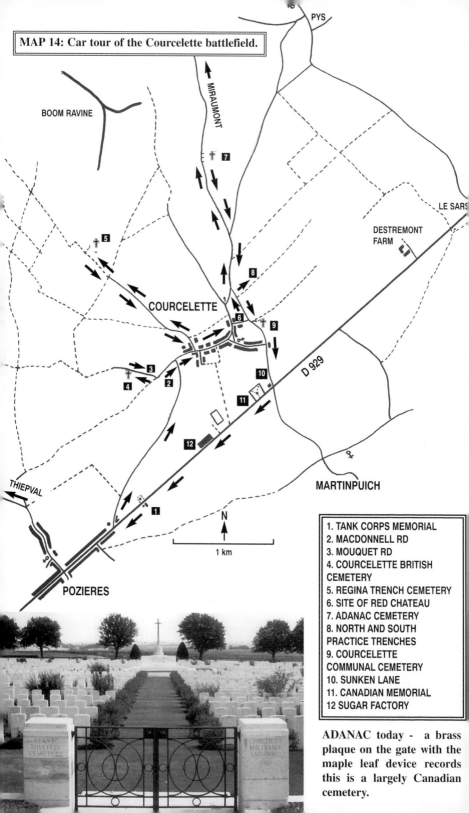

MAP 14: Car tour of the Courcelette battlefield.

PYS

BOOM RAVINE

MIRAUMONT

✝ **7**

LE SARS

DESTREMONT
FARM

✝ **5**

8

COURCELETTE

6

✝ **9**

D 929

3

10

4

2

11

12

MARTINPUICH

THIEPVAL

1

N

1 km

POZIERES

1. TANK CORPS MEMORIAL
2. MACDONNELL RD
3. MOUQUET RD
4. COURCELETTE BRITISH
CEMETERY
5. REGINA TRENCH CEMETERY
6. SITE OF RED CHATEAU
7. ADANAC CEMETERY
8. NORTH AND SOUTH
PRACTICE TRENCHES
9. COURCELETTE
COMMUNAL CEMETERY
10. SUNKEN LANE
11. CANADIAN MEMORIAL
12 SUGAR FACTORY

ADANAC today - a brass
plaque on the gate with the
maple leaf device records
this is a largely Canadian
cemetery.

Chapter Seven

A GUIDE TO THE COURCELETTE
BATTLEFIELD TODAY

1. Touring The Courcelette Battlefield by Car

This tour will take less than a couple of hours, depending on how much time you spend in the various cemeteries, and can easily be fitted into part of a more general visit to the Somme Battlefields, perhaps in conjunction with suggested tours in other *Battleground Europe* publications.

Start the tour at the Pozieres Windmill site on the main Albert-Bapaume road (D.929). This is easily reached from any part of the Somme battlefield. Here the 2nd Australian Memorial and **Tank Corps Memorial** can be visited. Located on the site where Captain Inglis' tank left for the attack on the Sugar Factory, this is the only Great War memorial to the tanks on the Western Front. It takes the form of a large plinth surrounded by four bronze models of Great War tanks. Six-pounder guns and tank driving chain form the boundary fence. Opposite is a memorial to the 2nd Australian Division, who captured this ground, located on the actual site of Pozières Windmill. There are superb views from here across the ground before Courcelette and the Sugar Factory and using one of the trench maps reproduced elsewhere an appreciation of the ground facing the Canadian Corps can be obtained from here.

Tank Corps Memorial

Leaving the Pozières Memorial return towards Pozières village itself and turn right down a minor road signposted to Courcelette. It is quite a sharp turn. Here you are following the direction of the attack by 6th Brigade; the 27th Bn advanced to the left of the road and the 21st Bn towards the Sugar Refinery on the right. Good views of Courcelette and the lie of the ground are obtained as you go further along. Follow this road until a sharp bend just outside Courcelette is reached. Here turn sharp left, following the CWGC sign. You are now on **Macdonnell Road**. West of the village, this was the road, partly sunken in places, that runs from Courcelette to Pozières. It was named after Brigadier-General A.H. MacDonnell CMG DSO, commanding 5th Brigade, and also had a trench that followed the track on its southern edge. It was captured by the 42nd Bn and the PPCLI on 15th September 1916. One of C Company Heavy Section Machine Gun Corps Mark I tanks came unstuck near this road on the same day, being abandoned by its crew. After the fighting had moved beyond Zollern Graben, units of the Canadian Field Artillery set up gun positions in the valley close to MacDonnell Road. In winter months this track can be muddy and flooded. Continue until a fork is reached; take the right hand fork and you will then be on Mouquet Road. In the same area, this is the sunken lane which runs from Courcelette to Mouquet Farm, the banks of which once contained many dugouts. It was swept up by the 42nd Bn and PPCLI on 15th September 1916 during their advance on Fabeck Graben which ran just to the north of this track. The 49th Bn entered the sunken lane later that night and it was close to here that Private J.C. Kerr won his Victoria Cross on 16th September.

Courcelette British Cemetery in the early 1920s.

Soon you will come to **Courcelette British Cemetery**. This cemetery is located in the old Mouquet Road and was originally known as Sunken Road Cemetery, owing to its location. Burials were made from November 1916 to March 1917; seventy-four soldiers were laid to rest in what is now Plot I. After the war many graves were brought in from the Pozières-Courcelette battlefields and the existing cemetery was made. The number of burials now total: 780 Canadian, 657 British, 514 Australian, one New Zealand, and four whose unit is not known. Of these 1,956 graves, some 1,177 are men whose identity is not known – over sixty percent. Of particular interest is the grave of Lieutenant J.C. Mewburn of the 18th Bn Canadian Infantry (Special Memorial I-A), who fell on 15th September 1916, aged twenty-two. His father, Major General S.C.Mewburn, was Minister of Militia and Defence in Canada. There are many very young soldiers also buried here; Private George Ritchie of the Royal Canadian Regiment died on 16th September 1916 aged only sixteen – he had joined up a year and a half before (II-A-20). Take time to visit the cemetery and

Courcelette from the air looking east. JOHN GILES

climb the banks of the sunken road opposite; Fabeck Graben ran just in front of you and from here there is good observation across the ground towards Courcelette on the right, and Zollern Graben which was further ahead of you.

Return to the road junction and go into **Courcelette Village**. Courcelette was a small farming village in August 1914, flanked to the south on the Albert-Bapaume road by a large Sugar Factory. After initial fighting between the French and Germans around Thiepval, the front line on this part of the Somme stabilised and Courcelette became an area for billeting German troops. Artillery batteries made good use of the many valleys around the village, and the ancient tunnels below Courcelette were taken over. A German cemetery was established alongside the pre-war civilian graves, and the village remained in good condition until the summer of 1916 when Australian troops were attacking Pozières. Battalions of the Canadian Expeditionary Force (CEF) successfully assaulted Courcelette on 15th September 1916, when tanks were used for the first time. The village was captured and the fighting moved to the high ground that surrounded Courcelette to the north and east. Courcelette was totally rebuilt in the 1920s and today there are only 142 villagers in this small farming community. The first house on the way into Courcelette from Pozières is 'Sommecourt'; where the author's wife runs a bed and breakfast establishment. Visitors are always welcome even if they are only just passing by, and there is a small collection of battlefield relics found in the Courcelette area on display. Sadly there are no shops or bars in Courcelette, the nearest being 'Le Tommy' in Pozières (see 'Advice for Travellers').

Now take the first turning to the left; initially a sunken road which then takes you over the high-ground. Follow the CWGC sign and continue for about a mile to a cross-road of tracks. Park your vehicle here and follow the track ahead down to **Regina Trench Cemetery**. Regina Trench was the longest named trench on the Western Front and was the scene of terrible and costly fighting from October 1916 to the close of the Battle of the Somme in November. The cemetery was started in the winter of 1916/17 and then contained 179 graves, ninety-seven of which were Canadian. After the war some 2,086 burials were brought into the cemetery from the Courcelette, Grandcourt and Miraumont areas. Total burials are now: 1,667 British, 563 Canadian, thirty-five from Australia and one American. The American was a pilot in the Royal Air Force, Lieutenant Ervin Shaw who was killed in aerial combat on 9th July 1918, aged twenty-four (IX-A-9). His Sergeant-Observer is buried with him. There are also many men from units of the 18th (Eastern) Division which attacked Boom Ravine – visible to the north-east from the cemetery gate – on 17th February 1917 in the last major engagement on the Somme. The trench itself ran at angles to the south of the cemetery, but there is no sign of it today. Many shells, grenades and trench mortar bombs turn up here in the ploughing months and should be left well alone.

Return to Courcelette village via the same route and turn left along Grande Rue towards the village war memorial. Beyond the memorial and just before the church, turn left down a minor road. After about two hundred yards take the first right and beyond the first house on the left stop. There is a good view across the fields here where **Red Chateau** once stood. Now only a field with a pronounced rise, presumably where the main chateau once stood, Red Chateau was a large building with huge cellars which could house between 300-400 men. In ruins by 1916, the Germans had used it as a field hospital up to the capture of Courcelette, when the Canadians implemented it for the same purpose and it was they who named it Red Chateau – possibly due to the colour of the brickwork. During ploughing time many such bricks are found in the field, but there is no sign of an entrance to the cellars which must surely remain. Also visible from here to the right is **The Quarry**. This position to the north-east of Courcelette was captured on the 15th September 1916 and became part of the front line for several weeks. One account mentions a German sniper in the steeple of Courcelette church firing on Canadian soldiers in the quarry two days or more after the capture of the village. He was swiftly dealt with! Around the quarry it is still possible to see evidence of shell holes and trenches.

Carry on along this minor road to the main Miraumont road and turn left towards Miraumont and continue until **ADANAC Cemetery** is reached. There was only one grave on this site at the close of the war, and the cemetery was created by concentrating many smaller burial sites in the Courcelette area and beyond. The name was made by spelling CANADA backwards. Today there are over 3,000 graves; 1,973 British, 1,071 Canadian, seventy New Zealand, fifty-three Australian and five whose unit is not known. The unnamed graves are 1,712 in number. Two Victoria Cross winners are buried here; Piper James Richardson of the Canadian Scottish, killed 9th October 1916, aged twenty (III-F-36), and Sergeant Samuel Forsyth of the New Zealand Engineers, who died on 24th August 1918, aged twenty-five – a veteran of Gallipoli (I-I-39). Other interesting Canadian graves are; Major A. Miln, second in command of the 75th Bn Canadian Infantry (I-H-28) and two sixteen year olds: Private Russell Lewis Collingridge, 3rd Bn who died on 8th October 1916 and was a native of Guelph, Ontario (VI-C-3), and Private Joseph Lorne Dewart, 87th Bn (Grenadier Guards of

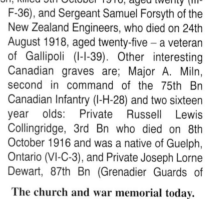

The church in mid-1916. TOM GUMSTEAD

The church and war memorial today.

Original wooden grave markers at ADANAC Cemetery in 1919.

Canada), killed 21st/22nd October 1916 (I-D-39). There are good views across the battlefield and Regina Trench ran very close to the southern border of the cemetery.

Return towards Courcelette and just before the quarry, take a minor road to the left. This will lead you into a valley where the **North & South Practice Trenches** were. These were sited either side of the valley which runs due east from the Courcelette-Miraumont Road. Constructed in 1915 to train German soldiers in trench raiding, they became a key feature in the fighting east of Courcelette. Piper James Richardson of the Canadian Scottish, won his VC in this area. There is no sign of these trenches today, although the valley itself is exactly as it was in 1916.

Go back to the Miraumont road and turn left. Just before the village take another minor road to the left. Up a steep bank is Courcelette communal cemetery and the **German Gravestone**. This gravestone, of Lieutenant Hermann Meyer, who was killed at Thiepval in December 1914, is the last remaining stone from the old Courcelette German Cemetery. The burial ground was located to the left of the current communal cemetery and remains of the brick entrance can also be seen. By 1916 there were 1,100 German graves. Among them were three British soldiers who now have a Special Memorial in Delville Wood Cemetery, Longueval. The German cemetery was destroyed in the fighting for Courcelette, and never reconstituted. One presumes the graves are still there today – now under a cultivated field. Inside the cemetery itself is an **Imperial War Graves Commission Headstone**. Located in the left plot, half-way towards the back of the cemetery, is a grey stone similar to the headstones found in military cemeteries. It records Frank A.H. Hayward, who worked for the Imperial War Graves Commission in the Courcelette area and died on 20th December 1936. During the Great War he had served as a Private in the Royal Sussex Regiment.

German gravestone, Courcelette Communal Cemetery

Once more, returning to the Miraumont road, follow it past the eastern entrance to Courcelette. Stop here in the **Sunken Road**. The Somme is well known for its sunken roads, and this one running south from Courcelette across the Albert-Bapaume road to Martinpuich, is perhaps the most famous on this part of the battlefield. It was entered by Canadian troops on 15th September, but not properly occupied until the next day. Lance Cattermole's 21st Bn was here that day and he gives a harrowing account of conditions in Chapter Two. It is nowhere near its original depth, but is still sunken. Nearby is the old Cafe of Le Baillon. This was built in the 1920s and Graham Seaton Hutchison in

The Canadian Memorial in the 1920s.

Pilgrimage, a 1930s guide to the battlefields, recommends it as a place for a good lunch and liquid refreshment. Today it is a private house.

Continue to where the Sunken Road meets the main Albert-Bapaume road and turn right. Just on the right is the **Canadian Memorial**. This memorial is one of a number which commemorate the battlefields of the Canadian Expeditionary Force in the Great War. It forms a grey stone block, inscribed with information about Canadian losses on the Somme, surrounded by gardens. There is also a visitors book inside a bronze locker bearing the maple leaf device.

Further up along the same road, also on the right, you will find the **Sugar Factory**. The Sugar Factory, or Refinery, was a key German position to the south of Courcelette and was captured by tanks and the 21st Bn Canadian Infantry on 15th September 1916. Huge cellars and tunnels made it a formidable defensive work. Today it is a garden centre open to the public, and can be freely visited. In the grounds is the old well – all that remains of the original sugar factory. Local stories suggest that the Germans ran pipes from this well to Mouquet Farm and other water points in the Courcelette area.

Staying on the D.929, within minutes you will return to the Pozières Windmill where the tour began. From here further cemeteries in Chapter Eight can easily be visited. Refreshments are found in Pozières at 'Le Tommy' bar, and Albert and the Musee des Abris Somme Museum is only ten minutes away. The Delville Wood Visitors' Centre is fifteen minutes from here, and the Historial Museum at Peronne about a forty-five minute journey across the 1916 battlefields.

2. Walking The Courcelette Battlefield

Like many other areas on the Somme, Courcelette is ideal for walking with many quiet tracks and country lanes. For ease of understanding the battlefield has been split up into three walks covering small areas which can be walked in a few hours. Details of the route are given, and where no specific details are given the text in bold refers to information given in the car tour section above.

Remains of the Sugar Factory.

WALK 1: THE 15TH SEPTEMBER 1916 ADVANCE

Park your vehicle at the **Tank Corps Memorial** opposite the Pozières Windmill site. Go across the main Albert-Bapaume road to the Australian Memorial. The Canadian front line was close to here on 15th September and there are good views across the ground towards Courcelette where the Canadian Corps attacked that day. From here return along the Albert-Bapaume road towards Pozières, keeping to the grass verge on the right, away from the busy traffic. Just pass a water tower and some houses, turn right down a minor road signposted for Courcelette and continue for some distance. You are roughly following the advance of the 27th Bn on the left, and 21st Bn, right- see Chapter Two. Where the road reaches the outskirts of Courcelette, on a sharp bend, turn left down a track, **Macdonnell Road**, which is also signposted for **Courcelette British Cemetery**. This is reached by taking another track to the right, further along Macdonnell Road – **Mouquet Road**.

From the cemetery return via the tracks into Courcelette and follow Grande Rue past 'Sommecourt' (on the left) and the junction for Regina Trench Cemetery, and take a minor road on the right, Rue Monette. Follow this to the end where there are good views back across to the Pozières Windmill. Turn left on this road which becomes a track and, after two hundred yards, turn right down a tree-lined avenue. Follow this to the Albert-Bapaume road, and turn left to reach the Canadian Memorial, again staying on the grass verge to avoid the traffic. From the memorial looking back to Pozières you have a good view to Pozières over the ground where the 20th Bn attacked Gun Pit Trench on 15th September; see Chapter Two.

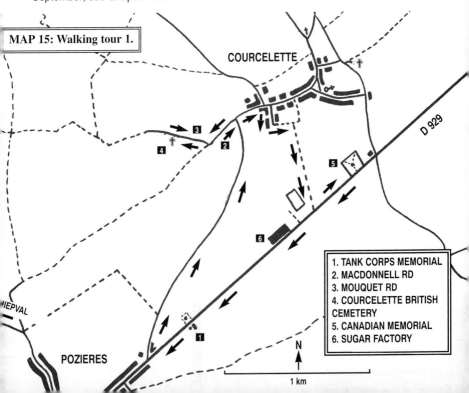

MAP 15: Walking tour 1.

COURCELETTE

D 929

NIEPVAL

POZIERES

N

1 km

1. TANK CORPS MEMORIAL
2. MACDONNELL RD
3. MOUQUET RD
4. COURCELETTE BRITISH CEMETERY
5. CANADIAN MEMORIAL
6. SUGAR FACTORY

Courcelette from the air, looking west. JOHN GILES

Leaving the memorial, return along the Albert-Bapaume Road until the **Sugar Factory** is reached on the right. Stop here to see the ground where Inglis' tanks advanced. From here is is a short walk back to the Tank Corps Memorial.

WALK 2: COURCELETTE LEFT SECTOR

Park your vehicle at **Courcelette British Cemetery**. After visiting the graves, turn left on the track, **Mouquet Road**, in the direction of Thiepval. This will bring you up on to some high ground and to your left the trees of Mouquet Farm are visible. Soon another track to the right appears – this was Twenty Three Road and Zollern Trench ran across here – see Chapter Three. Follow

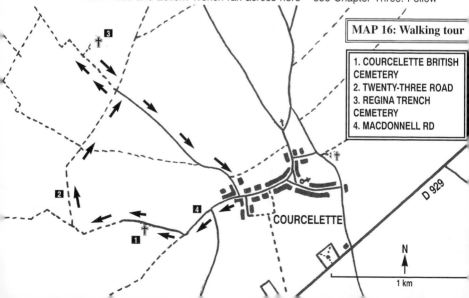

MAP 16: Walking tour

1. COURCELETTE BRITISH CEMETERY
2. TWENTY-THREE ROAD
3. REGINA TRENCH CEMETERY
4. MACDONNELL RD

COURCELETTE

N

1 km

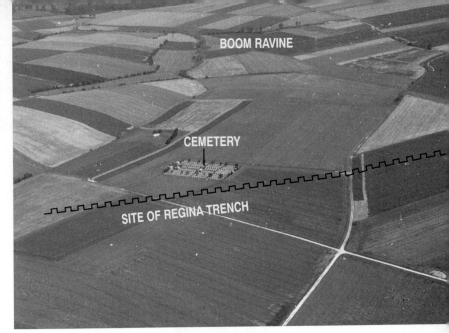

BOOM RAVINE

CEMETERY

SITE OF REGINA TRENCH

An aerial view of Regina Trench Cemetery. JOHN GILES

this across the fields until a cross-roads of tracks is reached. Turn left and continue downhill to **Regina Trench Cemetery**.

From the cemetery return to the cross-roads of tracks and go straight across. There are good views down into the village ahead of you and **Courcelette** is soon reached via a sunken lane, which Will Bird mentions in his account – see Chapter Six. In Courcelette turn right and go out of the village until a sharp bend is reached where Pozières is signposted to the right. Continue straight on down a track, **Macdonnell Road**, which will return you to Courcelette British Cemetery and your vehicle.

WALK 3: COURCELETTE RIGHT SECTOR

Park your vehicle in the village square near the war memorial and church in the centre of **Courcelette**. Follow Grande Rue towards Pozières and past the Mairie; a minor road signposted for Regina Trench Cemetery appears on the right. Follow this gradually uphill; Kenora Trench was over on the right up the slope. At a cross-roads of tracks go straight across and downhill to **Regina Trench Cemetery**.

Return to the cross-roads of tracks and turn left along Twenty-Three Road. After a few hundred yards the track forks; follow the right hand fork. This roughly follows the line of Regina Trench- see Chapter Four for details of the fighting here. Continue until the track meets another track and turn right, on a gradual slope downhill towards Courcelette. This was the West Miraumont

Road, and at the end near the crucifix (where shells are often dumped – beware!) was the jumping off point of the 31st Bn on 26th September 1916 – see Chapter Three. Continue up a minor road towards the village, then take a turning to the left. Past the second house on the left you can look back towards the crucifix. The immediate ground before you was the site of **Red Chateau**, and **The Quarry**, and **Dyke Road** can be seen over to the right. This was a minor road that ran east from the Miraumont Road down the valley between the North and South Practice Trenches. The banks of this valley were similar in appearance to dykes – thus the name.

Continue along the road and where it meets the main Miraumont road turn right then first left, and up a tarmac slope to Courcelette Communal Cemetery.

Red Chateau in mid-1916. TOM GUDMESTAD

Here a **German Gravestone** and **Imperial War Graves Commission Headstone** can be seen. Return to the Miraumont road and turn left into the **Sunken Road**, which is also mentioned by Will Bird in Chapter Six. Round a bend, a turning back into Courcelette appears on the right; follow this back to the war memorial and your vehicle.

MAP 17: Walking Tour 3.

1. VILLAGE SQUARE, COURCELETTE
2. REGINA TRENCH CEMETERY
3. TWENTY-THREE ROAD
4. WEST MIRAUMONT ROAD
5. CRUCIFIX
6. SITE OF RED CHATEAU
7. COURCELETTE COMMUNAL CEMETERY

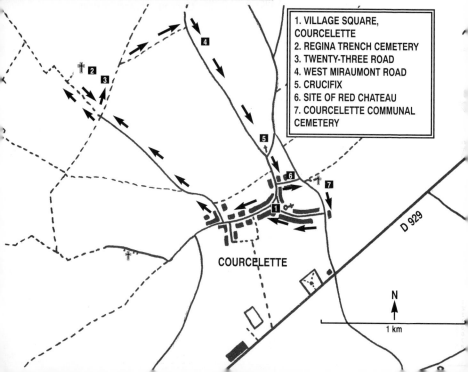

COURCELETTE

D 929

N

1 km

Chapter Eight

OTHER CANADIAN CEMETERIES ON THE SOMME

In addition to those mentioned in the guide to Courcelette above, there are many other cemeteries in the Somme area associated with the fighting at Courcelette and Regina Trench. Here only the military cemeteries connected with the Canadian operations between September and November 1916 are featured in this chapter. They are roughly in order of distance from Courcelette. There is also an entry for the Vimy Memorial, near Arras, which commemorates those Canadians who were killed in France and have no known grave: including those who fell on the Somme. *Sunken Road Cemetery, 2nd Canadian Cemetery, Sunken Road, Pozieres British Cemetery, Ovillers Military Cemetery, Bapaume Post Military Cemetery, Albert Communal Cemetery Extension, Warloy-Baillon Communal Cemetery Extension, Contay British Cemetery, Puchevillers British Cemetery, Serre Road No 1 & No 2 Cemeteries, AIF Burial Ground, Flers, Vimy Memorial.*

SUNKEN ROAD CEMETERY:

The Sunken Road, a common feature on the Somme battlefield, runs from Pozieres to Contalmaison and was formerly part of a wooded area known as 'Bois Defriches'. In winter time, and after rain, the access track is often impassable and it is wise to leave your vehicle by the Pozieres road and walk the rest of the way. The cemetery was started in July 1916, and used through

MAP 18: Canadian Cemeteries on the Somme. NAC

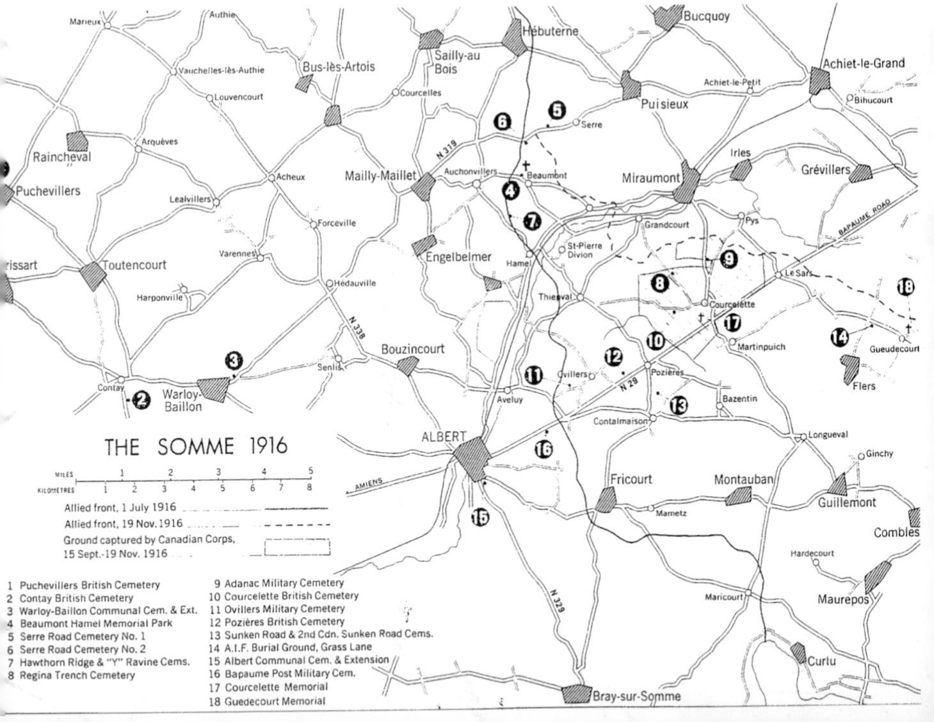

THE SOMME 1916

| MILES | 1 | 2 | 3 | 4 | 5 |
| KILOMETRES | 1 | 2 | 3 | 4 | 5 | 6 | 7 | 8 |

Allied front, 1 July 1916 ....
Allied front, 19 Nov. 1916 ...... – – – – –
Ground captured by Canadian Corps,
15 Sept.-19 Nov. 1916 ....

NAC

1 Puchevillers British Cemetery
2 Contay British Cemetery
3 Warloy-Baillon Communal Cem. & Ext.
4 Beaumont Hamel Memorial Park
5 Serre Road Cemetery No. 1
6 Serre Road Cemetery No. 2
7 Hawthorn Ridge & "Y" Ravine Cems.
8 Regina Trench Cemetery
9 Adanac Military Cemetery
10 Courcelette British Cemetery
11 Ovillers Military Cemetery
12 Pozières British Cemetery
13 Sunken Road & 2nd Cdn. Sunken Road Cems.
14 A.I.F. Burial Ground, Grass Lane
15 Albert Communal Cem. & Extension
16 Bapaume Post Military Cem.
17 Courcelette Memorial
18 Guedecourt Memorial

to October. Australians killed in the fighting at Pozieres were initially buried here, then Canadians as the battle moved on to Courcelette. Now there are 148 Canadian, sixty-one Australian and five British burials. Three Australian and one Canadian are unknown, and there are three Special Memorials.

A number of officers from the famous French-Canadian 22nd Bn ('Van-Doos') are buried in a row: Captain M.E. Bauset (II-D-4), Lieutenant A.P. Beaudry (II-D-6), Lieutenant L.R. Lavoie MM (II-D-5) and Major A.L.H. Renaud (II-D-3); all were killed between 15th-16th September 1916. Bauset's headstone inscription is entirely in French.

2ND CANADIAN CEMETERY, SUNKEN ROAD:

Located in the same sunken road as the previous cemetery, burials were made between September and October 1916. It is a regimental or 'comrades' cemetery containing forty-four graves exclusively from the 2nd Bn Canadian Infantry. Many such graveyards were closed after the war and moved into larger concentration cemeteries, and this is one of the few that still remain – and is one of the smallest on the 1916 Somme Battlefield, only just qualifying for a Cross of Sacrifice.

The 2nd Bn was one of the first CEF battalions on the Somme and fought in several actions around Pozieres and Courcelette. Close to the location of this cemetery they fought a costly action on 9th September 1916 (see Chapter 1). The battalion history records that in late September,

> "... small groups were sent to the scene of the action on September 9th to search for the bodies of some who had been reported missing. Among those found was that of Lieut H.C. Stuart." [1]

Lieutenant Henry Cuthbert Stuart was buried here (E-4); his grave is at the rear of the cemetery, slightly apart from the others.

POZIERES BRITISH CEMETERY:

Located on a site known in 1916 as Red Cross Corner and close to the Pozieres railway station, this cemetery was begun in July 1916 and the original graves are in Plot II. Many isolated burials and small cemeteries were brought in after the war, among them Casualty Corner Cemetery, Contalmaison, which contained twenty-one Canadian soldiers. Today, in addition to the 1,809 British,

Pnr E.C. Innes.

and 690 Australian graves, there are 218 Canadians. Of the overall total, the unknown number 1,374 and there are nineteen Special Memorials. The walls of Pozieres Cemetery form the Pozieres Memorial to the Missing, which commemorates 14,644 British soldiers who died in the German offensive on the Somme, March-April 1918.

Private Knud Olsen (III-Q-29) reflects the varied background of CEF soldiers; from Kristiansund in Norway, Olsen was killed on 15th September 1916 with the PPCLI. Pioneer E.C.Innes (II-F-5) of the 67th Canadian Pioneer Bn died on 22nd October 1916; his parents chose the following inscription: "Killed in Action, Battle of the Somme, For King and Country".

Another unusual inscription is on the grave of Private A.J.Burke (III-T-21) 38th Bn, killed in action 15th October 1916: "Allan is my name, Canada my nation, Ottawa my birthplace, Heaven my expectation".

OVILLERS MILITARY CEMETERY:

This is a large concentration cemetery, with many British graves from the opening phase of the Battle of the Somme. When it was created after the war, ninety-five Canadian graves were brought in from isolated burial sites in the Courcelette area. In total there are more than 3,500 soldiers buried at Ovillers – including some French 'Poilus' killed near La Boisselle-Ovillers in 1914-15. When some ground to the rear of the cemetery was cleared by a local farmer in 1982 he discovered the remains of forty-nine British and two German soldiers buried in a hap-hazard fashion in a large shell hole or old trench. None were identifiable by name, and they are now commemorated by a Special Memorial at Terlincthun Cemetery, near Boulogne.

BAPAUME POST MILITARY CEMETERY:

Located on the west side of Tara Hill, and south-west of Usna Hill, the cemetery was often known by these names during the war. Burials began after the 1st July 1916, when the divisions in action at La Boisselle and Ovillers buried their dead here. It remained in use until March 1917, by which time there were 152 graves which are now Plot I, Rows B-I. The cemetery fell into German hands in March 1918, when Albert was captured, and after the war 257 graves were brought in from the surrounding area.

The Canadians total sixty-four, the majority of which are from the Canadian Field Artillery, whose gun sites were in the La Boisselle area. Canon Scott's son was buried here after his grave was found near Regina Trench; Captain H.H.Scott (I-E-4). Nearby is the son of the Bishop of Quebec; Lieutenant J.W.Williams (I-I-7) was a brother officer of Captain Scott in the 87th Bn and died in the attack on Desire Trench 18th November 1916. In the same row are Majors F.E.Hall (I-I-2) and J.S.Lewis (I-I-3), also 87th Bn, who fell in the same action, as well as three officers from the 38th Bn. The youngest buried in Bapaume Post is Driver P.G.Layzell (I-H-6) who was killed on 14th November 1916, aged sixteen. Close by is possibly the last Canadian soldier to die on the Somme in 1916; Lieutenant B.H.A.Burrows (I-F-2), 12th Field Company Canadian Engineers, fell on 25th November 1916, just as the 4th Division was pulling out of Courcelette for the Vimy sector.

ALBERT COMMUNAL CEMETERY EXTENSION:

There were a number of Advanced Dressing Stations in operation at Albert before and during the Battle of the Somme, and burials from them were made here as early as August 1915. By November 1916 the 5th Casualty Clearing Station was also in Albert, and graves were added up to March 1917. The cemetery was used again in August 1918 and there are 618 British, 202 Canadian, thirty-nine Australian and two British West Indies burials here.

Canadian Field Ambulances used the cemetery throughout the fighting at

Courcelette and Regina Trench, but many officers killed at the front line were brought back here for burial. Among them are the three officers from the 13th Bn who were killed in their dugout at Courcelette on 26th September 1916: Lieutenant-Colonel V.C.Buchanan DSO (I-P-24), aged forty-seven, Captain C.C.Green (I-P-26) aged twenty-seven and Major W.F.Peterman (I-P-27) aged twenty-eight and who was also mentioned in dispatches. Lieutenant-Colonel R.P.Campbell (I-N-4) was the most senior medical officer to die at Courcelette. He was killed in the main street of the village while commanding 6th Field Ambulance Canadian Army Medical Corps. One account recalled,

> "... [he] *died half an hour after being struck in the right arm and under right collar bone by an explosive shell. The latter wound caused death by internal haemorrhage."* [1]

Major-General R.E.W.Turner VC CB DSO, commanding 2nd Division, attended his funeral in Albert the following day, along with many other senior Canadian officers.

WARLOY-BAILLON COMMUNAL CEMETERY EXTENSION:

Warloy-Baillon is on the main road from Arras to Amiens, and in September 1916 a Casualty Clearing Station was in operation here. Canadian wounded from Courcelette were brought to Warloy-Baillon between 15th-29th September 1916, and burials were made in Plot II during this period. A few graves were added later, and today there are 152 Canadian dead in the Cemetery Extension. Among them is the grave of Private F.H. Smith (II-B-7) of the 58th Bn, who died on 21st September, aged twenty-five. His parents, from the Channel Islands, later added on his headstone, "For King and Country, He Nobly Died, With Face to the Foe". The family of Sergeant C. Wilson (VI-B-18) of the 28th Bn, who died on 4th October, placed a private memorial on his grave during their visit here in the 1920s. It is still there today. There are very few Canadian officers buried in this cemetery.

CONTAY BRITISH CEMETERY:

Contay is a village some miles behind Albert where the 49th Casualty Clearing Station established itself in August 1916. The 9th CCS arrived in September,

Albert Communal Cemetery in 1919.

and from then onwards Canadians were buried here as they were evacuated wounded from the Pozieres-Courcelette battlefield. The graves were laid out on a gradual slope, and by the close of the Battle of the Somme there were 414 Canadians burials.

The graves are roughly in date order, starting in Plot I. The first burial was Private W.B. Bemister (I-B-2) of the 3rd Bn who died of wounds on 4th September 1916, aged eighteen, and was from Beverton, Ontario. The last Canadians to find their resting place here died on 29th November 1916 – over ten days after the Somme battle had ended. Others buried at Contay include Private Gustav Adolf Vic, who served as Weeks (I-F-3); he was an immigrant from Sweden who died with the 28th Bn on 3rd October 1916, aged twenty-nine. Some of the inscriptions are also worthy of mention. The parents of Private J.E. Stickers (IV-A-8), Royal Canadian Regiment, died of wounds 9th October 1916, chose, "He fell at the Somme, It is Immortal Honour". On the grave of Pte J.W. Aitkens, 18th Bn, one finds, " One of Canada's Best, Now Our Much Beloved Dead". Unusually, the officers are laid out in their own rows.

The Cross of Sacrifice at Warloy-Baillon.

PUCHEVILLERS BRITISH CEMETERY:

The 3rd and 44th Casualty Clearing Stations of the Royal Army Medical Corps arrived at Puchevillers – some distance from the front line – in June 1916 in readiness for the Somme offensive. They were busy all through the 1916 operations and Plots I-V of this cemetery, and most of Plot VI, are made up of casualties who died of wounds during this period. Burials continued until March 1917, and the cemetery was used again in March 1918. Further burials were made in August 1918, and today there are 1,132 British, 417 Australian, 213 Canadian and one New Zealand graves.

The majority of the 213 Canadians are men who died of wounds in September 1916, with a few from October. There are many pre-Courcelette casualties; the first Canadian burial is Lance Corporal C.Sevin (III-F-10) of Lord Strathcona's Horse who died of accidental injuries on 28th August 1916. The first battle casualty was Private F.E.Ventris (IV-A-11) of the 2nd Bn who died of wounds received at Pozières on 3rd September 1916. Private S.T.Hawkes (IV-C-22) has a small private memorial in front of his grave; he died on 14th September 1916 while serving with the 2nd CMR. The last CEF burial was Lance Corporal G.Plilkington (V-D-24) of the Canadian Corps Cavalry Regiment on 18th October 1916.

Like Contay, officers are buried in a separate row and there are only two Canadians among them: Lieutenant J.U.Garrow (III-A-14) of the 74th Bn died of wounds (gas) on 12th September 1916, and Lieutenant J.A.Hamilton MC (III-A-16) of the 27th Bn died aged thirty-six on 18th September 1916.

SERRE ROAD NO 1 AND NO 2 CEMETERIES:

Located some distance from Courcelette, these two large cemeteries nevertheless contain a large number of Canadian soldiers.

Serre Road No 1 is a concentration cemetery with graves from every sector of the 1916 Somme battlefield. Of the 2,412 burials and twenty-two Special

Memorials, 123 are Canadian and the majority unknown. Serre Road No 2 is the largest British cemetery on the 1916 Somme Battlefield with 7,139 graves of which 619 are Canadian; of this number 508 are unknown. Burials were made in this cemetery until after the Second World War, and the large number of soldiers who could not be positively identified gives some idea of the vast problem facing the Imperial War Graves Commission after the Great War.

AIF BURIAL GROUND, FLERS:

Another concentration cemetery, there are sixty-eight Canadian graves among the total of 3,581 British, Australian, New Zealand, South African and French dead. It originally got its name from the Australian Imperial Force (AIF) who buried their casualties here during the winter of 1916/17. Again, most of the Canadian graves are unknown but Private C.Boniface, who died with the 14th Bn on 7th September 1916, left a tragic story; he died almost a year to the day he was married in 1915.

VIMY MEMORIAL:

Pte C. Boniface.

About forty minutes by road from Courcelette, the Vimy Memorial is located on the crest of Hill 145 on Vimy Ridge, near Arras, and is part of a large memorial park to the Canadian victory in 1917. Trenches of both sides are preserved with concrete sandbags and duckboards, as are tunnels used by the Canadian Corps in the attack on the ridge in April 1917. These can be visited between April and November.

The memorial itself commemorates those Canadian soldiers who died in France between 1915 and 1918 who have no known grave. Designed by Walter S.Allward, the idea for the memorial came to him in a dream. Work started in 1925 but was not completed until 1936 when King Edward VIII came on 26th July to unveil it. A crowd of over 10,000 Canadians had made a special journey to attend the service of commemoration; with special boats, trains and buses. Among the guests of honour was Mrs Woods, who lost eight sons in the war. She came wearing all their medals and memorial crosses (Unique to the Canadians, this was a special silver cross issued to the mothers and widows of Canadian soldiers).

Of the 11,285 Canadian names the majority are men who died at Courcelette. There are many tragic stories, with over twenty sets of brothers listed on the walls. The registers also records a father and son, a Count, the grandson of the man who invented shrapnel, Black soldiers, Japanese immigrants who served in the CEF, and a soldier who had served as a Major in the British army at Gallipoli, been discharged and re-enlisted in the CEF only to be killed in action as a Private soldier. In many ways it is unique among the memorials to the missing in France and Flanders.

The names are listed in alphabetical order, and then by rank within each surname. A nearby visitors centre provides further information about the memorial and Vimy Ridge, and sells guide books and postcards. A new centre will be open by 1998, located close to the car park near the memorial.

FURTHER READING

General Works

Aitken, M. *Canada in Flanders: The Official Story of the Canadian Expeditionary Force, Volume I* (1916)

Beaverbrook, Lord *Canada in Flanders: The Official Story of the Canadian Expeditionary Force, Volume II* (1917)

Roberts, C.G.D. *Canada in Flanders: The Official Story of the Canadian Expeditionary Force, Volume III* (1918)

- These three books are the only contemporary 'official' history of the CEF and despite their faults remain useful eighty years later. The first two are widely available on the second-hand market, but the third is much rarer.

Nicolson, G.W.L. *Canadian Expeditionary Force 1914-1919* (The Queen's Printer 1962)

- This official history was considered too little, too late by many veterans, but is long overdue for reprinting. It now fetches high prices on the second-hand market.

Christie, N. *For King & Empire: The Canadians on the Somme- A Social History and Battlefield Tour* (CEF Books 1996)

- The only recent account of the CEF and part of a series detailing all the Canadian Battlefields in France and Belgium. Available at Delville Wood Visitors' Centre.

Giles, J. *The Somme Then & Now* (After The Battle 1986)

- This timeless book continues to inspire battlefield visitors old and new.

Gliddon, G. *When The Barrage Lifts* (Gliddon Books 1987)

- A useful topographical dictionary of the whole Somme Battlefield, despite its many errors. There are separate sections on Courcelette and Regina Trench.

McCarthy, C. *The Somme: The Day-By-Day Account* (Arms & Armour Press 1993)

- A condensed version of the British Official History (itself now being reprinted by the Imperial War Museum), the day by day activities of the Canadian Divisions are found here in the chapters for September-November 1916. Good maps - reprints from the OH.

Middlebrook, M. & M. *The Somme Battlefields* (Viking 1991).

- This classic guide to the Somme remains unrivalled and should be part of any serious visitor's library.

Pidgeon, T. *The Tanks at Flers* (By the author 1995)

- A highly detailed account of the first use of tanks in the Battle of Flers-Courcelette, with many unpublished photographs and a separate volume of facsimile trench maps. Recommended.

Memoirs

There are few published memoirs which cover the fighting at Courcelette.

Roy, R.H. (Ed) *The Journal of Private Fraser* (Sono Nis Press 1985)

- This superb book, extracts of which are quoted in this book, is one of the finest memoirs of the Great War. Hard to find in the UK, it is about to be reprinted by CEF Books in Canada.

Scott, F.G. *The Great War As I Saw It* (Goodchild 1922)

- An Army Chaplain who lost one of his sons at Courcelette, this is an honest account which deserves a wider audience.

Wheeler, V.W. *No Man's Land* (Calgary 1980)

- The author served with the 50th Bn at Courcelette. An interesting book, but one in need of editing.

SELECTIVE INDEX

142

86, 88, 118, 133
Kilpatrick, Rev G.G.D. 61
Loghrin, Mjr S.M. 35
Macdonnell Road 52, 125, 131,
    133
Macdonnell Trench 55-57
McLaughlin, Mjr A.E. 28-29

Memorials-
    Canadian 117, 130, 131
    2nd Australian 125
    Tank Corps 119, 125, 131,
    132
    Vimy 140
Mouquet Farm 22, 24-27, 52, 61,
    67, 78, 119, 125, 130
Mouquet Road 54, 58, 65, 125,
    131, 132
Munster Alley 28, 30
Musee des Abris 12, 130
North & South Practice Trenches
    84, 129, 134
Odlum, Brig-Gen V.W. 105
Parr, Mjr C.B. 82-84
Peck, Mjr C. 24-25
Pelly, Lr-Col R.T. 54-55
Pozieres 22, 24, 34, 49, 50, 52,
    100, 102, 109, 119, 125,
    127, 130, 131, 133
Quadrilateral, The 95
Quarry, The 128, 134
Red Chateau 128, 134
Regina Trench 31, 60, 67, 68, 69,
70, 73, 74, 78, 79-106, 107, 118
Roberts, Capt C.G.D. 115
Rosamund, Lt A.G. 67
Ross Rifle 15, 102
Salisbury Plain 17
Sausage Valley 27, 36, 76, 121
Scott, Canon 97-103, 105
Scott, Capt H.H. 97-103, 137

Stewart, Lt-Col C.J.T. 56-57, 61,
    66-67
Stuff Redoubt 70
Sugar Factory 34, 36-45, 48, 50,
    119, 125, 130, 132
Sugar Trench 45-48, 49-50, 52,
    55-56
Sunken Road 42-45, 129, 134
Swift, Lt-Col 27-28, 31
Thiepval Ridge, Battle of 67-78
Thomson, Lt-Col R.M. 89
Twenty Three Road 86, 88
Usna Hill 50, 54, 56, 121, 137
Valcartier Camp 15-16

Victoria Cross winners-
    Clarke, L. Cpl 27-32
    Fisher, F. L/Cpl 18
    Kerr, J.C. Pte 65-67, 125
    Richardson, J. Piper 92-95,
    128, 129
    Turner, Brig-Gen R.E.W. 18
Wheeler, Victor 111-115
Zollern Graben 57, 60, 61-67,
    68, 69, 70, 72, 73, 118, 125,
    127, 132
Zollern Redoubt 61